Policy Competition for Foreign Direct Investment

A Study of Competition among Governments to Attract FDI

By
Charles Oman

D1334857

DEVELOPMENT CENTRE
OF THE ORGANISATION FOR ECONOMIC CO-OPERATION AND DEVELOPMENT

ORGANISATION FOR ECONOMIC CO-OPERATION AND DEVELOPMENT

Pursuant to Article 1 of the Convention signed in Paris on 14th December 1960, and which came into force on 30th September 1961, the Organisation for Economic Co-operation and Development (OECD) shall promote policies designed:

- to achieve the highest sustainable economic growth and employment and a rising standard of living in Member countries, while maintaining financial stability, and thus to contribute to the development of the world economy;
- to contribute to sound economic expansion in Member as well as non-member countries in the process of economic development; and
- to contribute to the expansion of world trade on a multilateral, non-discriminatory basis in accordance with international obligations.

The original Member countries of the OECD are Austria, Belgium, Canada, Denmark, France, Germany, Greece, Iceland, Ireland, Italy, Luxembourg, the Netherlands, Norway, Portugal, Spain, Sweden, Switzerland, Turkey, the United Kingdom and the United States. The following countries became Members subsequently through accession at the dates indicated hereafter: Japan (28th April 1964), Finland (28th January 1969), Australia (7th June 1971), New Zealand (29th May 1973), Mexico (18th May 1994), the Czech Republic (21st December 1995), Hungary (7th May 1996), Poland (22nd November 1996) and Korea (12th December 1996). The Commission of the European Communities takes part in the work of the OECD (Article 13 of the OECD Convention).

The Development Centre of the Organisation for Economic Co-operation and Development was established by decision of the OECD Council on 23rd October 1962 and comprises twenty-three Member countries of the OECD: Austria, Belgium, Canada, the Czech Republic, Denmark, Finland, France, Germany, Greece, Iceland, Ireland, Italy, Korea, Luxembourg, Mexico, the Netherlands, Norway, Poland, Portugal, Spain, Sweden and Switzerland, as well as Argentina and Brazil from March 1994, and Chile since November 1998. The Commission of the European Communities also takes part in the Centre's Advisory Board.

The purpose of the Centre is to bring together the knowledge and experience available in Member countries of both economic development and the formulation and execution of general economic policies; to adapt such knowledge and experience to the actual needs of countries or regions in the process of development and to put the results at the disposal of the countries by appropriate means.

The Centre has a special and autonomous position within the OECD which enables it to enjoy scientific independence in the execution of its task. Nevertheless, the Centre can draw upon the experience and knowledge available in the OECD in the development field.

Publié en français sous le titre :

QUELLE POLITIQUES POUR ATTIRER LES INVESTISSEMENTS DIRECTS ÉTRANGERS ?
Une étude de la concurrence entre gouvernements

 THE OPINIONS EXPRESSED AND ARGUMENTS EMPLOYED IN THIS PUBLICATION ARE THE SOLE RESPONSIBILITY OF THE AUTHOR AND DO NOT NECESSARILY REFLECT THOSE OF THE OECD OR OF THE GOVERNMENTS OF ITS MEMBER COUNTRIES.

*
* *

Foreword

This publication was undertaken in the context of the Development Centre's research programme on the policy challenges of globalisation.

Acknowledgements

The Development Centre and the author are particularly grateful to participants in the Centre's November 1998 meeting of experts on Policy Competition and Foreign Direct Investment, who provided valuable comments on a draft of this study, and to the authors of the country- and region-specific analyses on which this study relies heavily:

- John Bachtler and his team at the University of Strathclyde's European Policies Research Centre (Europe)
- Jaime Campos, Executive Director, *Fundación Invertir* (Argentina)
- Edward K.Y. Chen, President, Lignan College, Hong Kong (China)
- Chia Siow Yue, Director, Institute of Southeast Asian Studies (Singapore)
- Jack Donahue, Professor, John F. Kennedy School, Harvard University (United States)
- Hu Angang, Chinese Academy of Sciences (China)
- Weng-Jeng Kuo and Shin-Horng Chen, Chung-Hua Institution for Economic Research (Chinese Taipei)
- Michael Mortimore and Wilson Peres, UN Economic Commission for Latin America and the Caribbean (Caribbean Basin)
- Pedro Noyola and Enrique Espinosa, SAI Law and Economics (Mexico)
- André and Françoy Raynauld (Canada)
- Sieh Lee Mei Ling, Professor, University of Malaya (Malaysia)
- R. Venkatesan and colleagues at the National Council of Applied Economic Research (India)
- Pedro Da Motta Veiga and Roberto Iglesias (Brazil).

The Development Centre and the author are also grateful to Dale Weigel, General Manager of the Foreign Investment Advisory Service (World Bank Group), Ann Houtman, Head of State Aids at the Commission of the European Communities, and André Raynauld, Emeritus Professor of Economics at the University of Montreal, for their detailed comments on the manuscript, and to colleagues in the Trade Union Advisory Committee's Secretariat and in the OECD Directorates for the Environment, for Education, Employment, Labour and Social Affairs, and for Financial, Fiscal and Enterprise Affairs for their comments on and contributions to the study (whose responsibility nevertheless remains that of the Development Centre).

The author would also like to thank Gauri Sikri for her invaluable research assistance, and Teresa Wells and Sandra Lloyd for typing the manuscript.

Table of Contents

Preface

Globalisation poses numerous challenges for policy makers both in developing countries and emerging economies and in OECD Member countries. One of these challenges stems from a widespread concern that, as governments in developing and emerging economies move to adopt more open and market-friendly policy regimes, and seek more actively to attract the foreign direct investment which they see as vital to strengthening the ability of their economies to compete in global markets, they may stimulate or reinforce a global process of competition among governments to attract FDI that has undesirable effects. Of particular concern is the danger that such competition may lead governments to engage in "bidding wars" that drive up investment subsidies to exorbitant levels, and/or drive down public measures that are needed to protect the environment and/or workers' rights and labour standards.

This study seeks to address those concerns, and to shed light on the implications for developing and emerging economies of competition among governments worldwide to attract FDI. It argues that although such competition is indeed widespread, and can be very intense in particular industries or for particular investment projects, overall the competition for real long-term corporate investment has both positive and negative effects, and it is important not to overstate its net effects — in either direction. While the inherent difficulty to obtain reliable data particularly on the subsidies that investors actually receive makes any conclusion tentative (neither the governments that provide them nor the investors that receive them readily supply such information), the most damaging overall effects appear to stem less from the direct financial cost to governments of investment subsidies paid out, or from any lowering of environmental or labour standards, than from the lack of policy transparency and government accountability that the process of competition for FDI tends to engender. This lack of policy transparency and accountability creates significant possibilities for graft and corruption, and for rent-seeking behaviour more broadly, which can in turn be highly detrimental to the processes of developing competitive markets and sound policy-making — processes which are fundamental to development itself.

From a policy perspective, the study thus argues for the importance of encouraging governments to move away from incentives-based means of competing to attract FDI in favour of greater concentration on rules-based means of competing that do not weaken environmental and labour standards. It calls for national and international rules (the latter at the regional and perhaps multilateral levels) that create more stable, predictable and transparent rules for investors and governments alike. These rules should help governments collectively to overcome the "prisoner's dilemma" nature of policy competition, and the "free rider" problem associated with it, and should favour policies that work to enhance productivity growth in developing and emerging economies in ways that promote sustainable development and improved working conditions in those countries.

Undertaken as part of the follow-up to the Development Centre's work on globalisation, this study further highlights the fact that just as globalisation creates major challenges for policy makers in both developing countries and OECD countries, so is it important for governments in the two groups of countries to work together in responding to those challenges. Promoting stable, predictable and transparent rules to enhance the flow of FDI to developing countries is one important way to do that.

Ulrich Hiemenz
Director
OECD Development Centre
October 1999

Executive Summary

Globalisation, and in particular the move by many developing and emerging economies in recent years to seek more actively to attract foreign direct investment, is raising policy makers' concern that intensifying global competition among governments to attract FDI may have undesirable effects. The main concern is that global "bidding wars" to attract FDI may be producing an uncontrolled upward spiral in costly "investment incentives" that weaken public finances while introducing market distortions in the allocation of real investment, and/or that such "wars" are putting excessive downward pressure on global standards of protection of the environment and/or of workers' rights (the so-called "race to the bottom").

Intensifying global competition among governments to attract FDI could also, however, produce beneficial effects. These effects may include inducing governments to strengthen their economies' "fundamentals" (e.g. by pursuing policies to enhance the supply of modern infrastructure and appropriately trained workers, by achieving greater macroeconomic and political stability, by improving long-term economic growth perspectives) which should in turn promote economic development — almost independently of their impact on FDI flows *per se*. Another effect may be to increase the global supply of FDI, to the benefit of investors and host economies alike.

The actual degree of global competition to attract FDI is not known, moreover, and while there is considerable evidence that such competition is widespread, involving sub-national as well as national governments both in OECD countries and in developing and emerging economies, it is difficult to predict whether that competition will intensify in the coming years.

It is against this backdrop that the present study addresses three sets of questions: *i)* to what extent do governments — national and sub-national governments in OECD and non-OECD countries — actually compete with one another to attract FDI; to what extent is that competition intensifying, or likely to intensify; and what are the principal policy instruments or means by which governments compete to attract FDI? *ii)* what are the effects of that competition — on FDI flows, on policy-making more broadly, and on the economy? and *iii)* what are the implications for policy makers? The study addresses these questions from the dual policy perspective of enhancing economic and social development in the developing and emerging economies, and of strengthening relations between those economies and OECD Member countries.

9

Chapter 1 lays out the policy and conceptual issues and the working hypotheses that guide the study. Chapters 2 and 3 present the evidence. Chapter 2 looks at governments' use of financial and fiscal incentives ("incentives-based competition") while Chapter 3 focuses on governments' use of "rules-based" means of competing to attract FDI — means such as environmental and labour standards, export-processing zones, international regional-integration agreements, privatisation of state-owned enterprises and strengthened judicial systems. Chapter 4 concludes with a presentation of the overall findings and policy conclusions.

Those findings and conclusions may be summarised as follows:

— Incentives-based competition for FDI is a global phenomenon: governments at all levels (national and sub-national) in both OECD and non-OECD countries engage in it worldwide.

— As barriers to international investment have fallen over the last two decades, the significance of competition for FDI has increased.

— Incentives-based competition can be intense, but the evidence — which is insufficient to draw more than tentative inferences — suggests that the competition tends to be quite intense only in particular industries (e.g. automobiles) or for particular investment projects (especially large ones) and in some industries is intense only during particular periods.

— Most incentives-based competition is effectively intra-regional, since much of the real investment for which national and sub-national governments compete is investment the investor intends in principle to locate in a particular region.

— While the evidence does not clearly point to any inexorable tendency towards global "bidding wars" among governments in their competition to attract FDI, the "prisoner's dilemma" nature of the competition creates a permanent danger of such "wars".

— Data on the direct financial and/or fiscal "cost-per-job" of incentives received by investors in the automobile industry reveal similar orders of magnitude of that cost in OECD and in developing and emerging economies (a cost that often exceeds $100 000).

— Evidence of the effects of incentives on corporations' real investment-location decisions, particularly for major new investment projects, is consistent with the view that the decision is normally a two-stage (or multi-stage) process in which investors *first* draw up a short list of acceptable sites on the basis of the economic and political "fundamentals" of alternative sites, largely irrespective of the availability of fiscal and financial incentives from potential host governments, and only *later*, after the short list is drawn up on the basis of the investment "fundamentals", do investors consider — and often seek out — investment incentives, sometimes playing one government off another at this stage of their location decision. Incentives and other discretionary government policies to attract FDI can thus be decisive in investors' location decisions, despite the much greater overall importance investors attach to the "fundamentals".

— There is little evidence that increasing global competition for FDI over the last two decades has contributed in any significant way to the major growth of global FDI that has occurred over the same period. Rather, any relationship of cause and effect between the two phenomena appears more to work in the opposite direction: as the global supply of FDI has risen significantly, governments have intensified competition with one another to attract "their share" of that growth. (Several factors have stimulated the growth of FDI, including Europe's Single Market and Maastricht Accords and other regional phenomena, e.g. NAFTA, as well as worldwide economic policy liberalisation and market deregulation and the globalisation of corporate activity and competition.)

— Even in the absence of global bidding wars for FDI, the *distortionary* effects of incentives — which tend to discriminate against smaller firms, against local firms (*de facto*, though rarely on a *de jure* basis) and against firms in sectors or types of activity that are not targeted — can be significant.

— It can be counterproductive for a government to offer costly investment incentives if the "fundamentals" of the potential investment sites within its jurisdiction fail to meet serious long-term real investors' basic requirements, because the incentives — in addition to the distortions they inevitably introduce — will tend to attract the "wrong kind" of investor. They also tend to render the broader policy-making process more vulnerable to rent-seeking behaviour, perhaps including corruption, which can be very costly — and can even spread and become quite destructive for the economy, for democracy and the development of a modern state, and thus for the very process of development.

— Undiscerning use of investment incentives and other discretionary policies by governments to attract FDI can have a negative effect on FDI inflows, in part, because the incentive programmes and policies tend to be seen by investors as unsustainable.

— Many of the governments that are most successful in attracting FDI are also among those that best meet the requirements for good governance (requirements that include sound public finances because they lend credibility to incentives programmes in the eyes of investors, and legitimacy in the eyes of voters, by making them likely to be seen as sustainable).

— There is little evidence to support the hypothesis that intensifying competition to attract FDI induces governments significantly to enhance local supplies of infrastructure and of skilled labour; one cannot reject the hypothesis that incentives tend more to compete with than to augment the use of public resources to increase local productivity-enhancing human-capital formation and the supply of modern infrastructure.

— Whether or not induced by competition to attract FDI, policies to enhance local supplies of human capital and modern infrastructure, if successful, *can* nevertheless be a powerful means to attract FDI — as well as to promote economic development — if the other "fundamentals" are sound.

— While governments often "justify" providing investment incentives with the argument that they are needed to steer corporate investment to poorer areas within their economy, in practice incentives are often of limited effectiveness in this regard (though there are exceptions) and they sometimes actually reinforce inequalities instead.

— Competition for FDI among sub-national governments has been "activitated" by, but also contributes to, a broader process of reform of policy-making which includes regulatory reform, privatisation and liberalisation of trade and investment policies. In addition to strengthening market forces, this process tends to induce sub-national governments to modernise and organise themselves better, and more flexibly, to enhance the competitiveness of the economies under their jurisdiction.

— Investors often choose sites where the host government's strategy to attract investors is part of a broader process of mobilisation around a project of social and political reform in which the government redefines its role, turning away from rigid structures and exclusive relationships with vested interest groups in favour of greater transparency, democracy and market competition. This process both enhances and is reinforced by growing exposure of local and foreign firms in the domesic market to international competition.

— Policy competition raises the delicate question of how to ensure the *accountability* of government officials, particularly those involved in the negotiation of discretionary incentive packages, and points up the need for governments to be able to monitor their own use of incentives. That monitoring could in turn constitute the needed basis for co-operation among governments to ensure that competition for FDI does not lead to beggar-thy-neighbour policy competition and incentives "bidding wars".

— There is little evidence in support of the stronger versions of the "race to the bottom" hypotheses regarding governments' defense of labour and environmental standards. The evidence cannot tell us, however, to what extent competition to attract FDI is inhibiting a socially optimal *raising* of those standards, and the danger of such "races"— or at least of increasing downward pressures on those standards — always exists. There is, at the same time, evidence that competition to attract FDI can exert some *upward* pressure on those standards, particularly by local governments.

— Policy makers must remain vigilant to ensure that competition to attract FDI does not lower labour and environmental standards but works, if anything, in the opposite direction. Governments and society would benefit in this regard from enhanced international policy co-ordination on environmental standards, perhaps also on *core* labour standards.

— International regional-integration agreements can be a powerful policy tool both for attracting FDI (which requires relatively *open* regional agreements) and for enhancing co-operation among governments to limit the potential negative effects of policy competition — including downward pressures on labour and environmental standards as well as costly beggar-thy-neighbour policy wars and incentive wars.

— For developing and emerging economies, whose scarce financial resources often push them into a heavy reliance on fiscal incentives to attract FDI, it is important to stress the value of moving away from discretionary incentives towards greater reliance on *rules-based* means of attracting FDI — national and international rules that maintain or strengthen environmental and labour standards and create stability, predictability and transparency for policy makers and investors alike. A strong rules-based approach, which should include a strong and independent judiciary system, can also provide the policy transparency necessary to limit the rent-seeking behaviour that can be very damaging to development.

— The prisoner's-dilemma nature of competition for FDI creates a permanent risk of costly beggar-thy-neighbour bidding wars and downward pressure on environmental and labour standards that cannot be fully addressed by national governments in the absence of strengthened international policy co-ordination.

Chapter 1

The Phenomenon, The Debate

Competition among governments to attract corporate investment appears to have heated up in recent years.

One reason for this is the large number of developing and emerging market economies — comprising three-quarters of humanity — that have moved during the 1980s and 1990s from relatively closed state-led growth strategies and *dirigiste* policy regimes to more open and market-friendly policy regimes, and have moved in the process to seek actively to attract foreign direct investment. China alone, for example, has moved from a policy of virtually excluding FDI, until 1979, to successfully attracting an annual FDI inflow of over \$40 billion by the mid-1990s — and in doing so has caused developing and emerging countries throughout Asia, and beyond, to worry about intensifying competition, with China and with each other, to attract FDI. The crisis that emerged in Asia in 1997 has tended, if anything, only to heighten those worries.

A second important reason why the competition appears to have heated up is that OECD governments have also moved in the 1980s and 1990s towards more reliance on markets. This move, led by market deregulation and further liberalisation of policies on international trade and capital flows, was launched largely as a policy response to the marked slowdown of productivity growth in the OECD economies in the 1970s and the emergence of "stagflation" (high unemployment, caused by slow growth, combined with high inflation) that followed in the late-1970s in North America and Europe. One consequence of this move, in a policy context increasingly oriented towards "competitiveness", has been a tendency by governments in North America (notably state governments in the United States and provincial governments in Canada) and by governments in Europe (national and sub-national governments) to seek more actively to attract corporate investors — foreign and domestic — as a means to create jobs and strengthen the local economy.

Together, the sea change in economic policy orientation in the developing and emerging market economies (including in Central and Eastern Europe) and the moves in OECD countries to deregulate markets and liberalise policies — with significant privatisation of state-owned enterprises undertaken in both groups of countries — have drawn national and sub-national governments' attention, worldwide, to the indispensable role of real private investment as an engine of growth and as a source of jobs and competitive strength.

The impact of these policy changes and enhanced attention to the importance of promoting corporate investment, in terms of fomenting inter-governmental competition to attract FDI, has in turn been amplified by "globalisation" — also a phenomenon of the 1980s and 1990s — which has increased the pressures of competition felt by governments, as well as by firms and workers. Particularly important, in this regard, is the extent to which globalisation has increased the *mobility* of capital, making it easier for a prospective investor to play potential host governments off against one another in their bids to attract, or perhaps retain, a major investment project[1].

Little is known, however, about the effects of intensifying competition among governments to attract FDI — or even about the degree to which such competition is actually intensifying, or likely to intensify in the coming years. Whether seen from the perspective of promoting economic development in today's developing countries or from that of enhancing relations between OECD countries and developing countries — the two perspectives of this study — the issue is nevertheless important and politically sensitive. One reason is because of the importance of FDI for economic development, and of the efforts now being undertaken in developing countries and emerging economies to attract it. Another reason is that, rightly or wrongly, many people, including many in OECD countries, believe that as developing and emerging economies compete more aggressively to attract investment by firms based in OECD countries, they are driving an intensification of competition by governments worldwide — in OECD as well as in non-OECD countries — to attract such investment. Many fear that the pressures of this competition are driving governments in OECD (and non-OECD) countries to engage in cut-throat bidding wars to attract FDI — wars they fear are weakening governments' will, or ability, to enforce necessary public standards of protection of the environment and of workers' rights, and/or leading governments to offer corporate investors excessive fiscal and financial subsidies in the form of investment incentives.

The apparent intensification of competition among governments worldwide to attract corporate investment is thus often blamed, rightly or wrongly, on the growing openness of developing and emerging economies and, in particular, their growing efforts to attract FDI by OECD-based investors. The effects of such competition on the economies of the developing and emerging economies are poorly understood. On both counts, research on this issue requires a careful empirical examination of the patterns and effects of the competition for FDI by governments in both OECD and developing countries — particularly, among the latter, in Latin America and Asia, which are the regions that attract the bulk of FDI that goes to developing and emerging economies.

Two Interpretations

While the dangers of excessive competition among governments to attract FDI have generated considerable concern, such competition may also produce benefits. To guide our empirical analysis, it is therefore important conceptually to consider both sides of the picture.

Positive-sum Game Hypothesis

On the positive side are interpretations that can be called "positive-sum game" scenarios, because they portray inter-governmental competition to attract FDI as producing net benefits for investors and host economies alike.

These interpretations build on the observation, largely confirmed by interviews with corporate managers, that investors, when selecting the site for a major investment project, tend to attach much greater importance to the so-called "fundamentals" — political and macroeconomic stability, market access and long-term growth potential, the availability of appropriately skilled workers and of necessary infrastructure — than they do to receiving fiscal or financial incentives from the prospective host government[2]. This priority is particularly true for investors that are planning a major long-term investment in the creation or expansion of production capabilities, perhaps using advanced technologies, etc., i.e. for the kind of investment that governments most want to attract.

The reasoning is that, because governments know, or should know, the high priority investors attach to the "fundamentals" relative to fiscal and financial incentives, an intensification of competition among governments to attract investment can be expected to induce governments to focus on improving the "fundamentals". Governments responding to intensifying competition will thus seek to improve domestic supplies of human capital and infrastructure, in particular, as well as to ensure political and macroeconomic stability. The effect of intensifying inter-governmental competition should thus be to lead governments to take actions that will strengthen their economies, to the benefit of their own firms and workers — even if, ultimately, those actions do not actually attract much additional FDI (say, because all countries do likewise)!

The power of the argument is enhanced, moreover, by the fact that investments both in human capital formation (education, training, etc.) and in infrastructure have significant "public good" characteristics. This means that market forces, on their own, will tend to produce a sub-optimal level of investment in both. In competing to attract FDI, governments may increase that level either directly, through increased public investment in the supply of human capital formation and/or infrastructure, or indirectly, through measures to induce more private investment in their supply. The important point is that more intense competition among governments to attract FDI can be expected, according to this interpretation, to lead governments to do one or the other (or both) to a degree they would not have done in the absence of such competition. Such competition may also give governments more incentive to increase the *efficacy* of whatever investment goes into human capital formation and infrastructure.

By providing the stimulus some governments need to increase the level and efficacy of investment in human capital formation and infrastructure, according to this interpretation, competition among governments to attract FDI can thus be expected to raise productivity levels of domestic capital and labour, as well as of foreign capital, while bringing the level of investment in human capital and infrastructure closer to the socially optimal level. It can also work to enhance political and macroeconomic stability — in individual countries, and worldwide.

A corollary hypothesis of the positive-sum game line of interpretation is that as competition among governments to attract investment heats up, and leads governments to "do a better job on the fundamentals", the total volume of investment and FDI, worldwide, will grow. Moreover, it is noted, FDI as a whole can have important "public good" characteristics in the sense that it can produce important benefits in the host economy which are not captured by the investor — so-called "spillover effects". These benefits range from local learning effects (derived, for example, from domestic firms' imitation of foreign investors' practices, from labour and managerial mobility between foreign-owned and domestic firms, and/or from supplier relationships) to enhanced competition in the local market — competition that pressures local firms to modernise, improve product quality, seek-out new technologies, become more efficient, reduce prices, etc.

Thus, in addition to inducing governments individually and collectively to pursue actions that enhance their economies' growth and productivity levels even in the absence of additional FDI, according to the positive-sum game interpretation, those actions are likely to induce an increase in the global supply of investment and FDI — independently of the extent to which investment is diverted from one country to another by those actions. Also, because FDI can produce significant spillover benefits for the host economy, this increase in global FDI brings up the level of global FDI from a sub-optimal level to one that is closer to socially optimal.

On all accounts, then, according to the positive-sum game interpretation, intensifying competition among governments to attract FDI should prove beneficial, on balance, both to investors and to governments, and to society as a whole.

Negative-sum Game Hypothesis

While the positive-sum game hypothesis points up the *potential* for FDI competition among governments to have the positive effects just described, it is equally plausible that, in practice, this potential tends to be offset — even overwhelmed — by the "prisoner's dilemma" created by the dynamics of the competition. The problem, according to this interpretation, is that as the competition heats up, governments come under increasing pressure to engage in costly "bidding wars" that leads them continually to increase the level of public subsidies offered to investors — fiscal and financial "incentives" — until that level far surpasses any that could possibly be justifiable from society's perspective (even taking account of the possible spillover benefits to be derived from additional global FDI). The "prisoner's dilemma" results from the fact that while governments have a collective interest in refraining from such bidding wars, individual governments engage in the bidding process because of the danger that if they refrain from doing so, FDI will be diverted from the economy under their jurisdiction to that of one that offers investors more incentives.

The negative-sum game line of reasoning builds on the observation, also largely confirmed by interviews with corporate managers, that while investors overwhelmingly attach more importance to the "fundamentals" than to "incentives" when selecting the site for a major long-term investment project, they also tend, in practice, to draw up a short list of preferred sites, any one of which would be acceptable in terms of the criteria the investor judges most important. Then, because these sites are commonly located in the jurisdiction of different governments (sub-national and/or national governments) it is common practice for investors to negotiate conditions and possible incentives with each government[3]. Investors may do so openly, to foment competition among the governments, or else "ask for their best offers", before making their final site selection.

While the pressures on governments to engage in bidding to attract FDI are thus intense, and easily understood, according to this interpretation, the extent of the costs and "distortions" or perverse effects they can cause is easily underestimated. One reason, relatively obvious, is that the public funds used to pay for incentives could often be used more productively — including to attract FDI, in the long run — by investing them in such public goods as human capital formation and infrastructure. Another reason, also important if less readily apparent, is that incentive programmes tend to put earlier, already-established investors (domestic as well as foreign) at a cost and thus competitive disadvantage relative to the "newcomer" investors that benefit from the incentives. The consequences can range from driving established investors to leave, or to engage in "round-tripping" (investing abroad in order to return as a "new" foreign investment), which are wasteful, to driving them into various corrupt practices, which can ultimately be even more damaging and costly.

A third reason, often invisible but very important, is the extent to which a government's extensive use of incentives — which may also lack transparency — will be seen by some of the most serious potential major long-term investors as unsustainable. Those perceptions often weaken such investors' faith in the stability and credibility of government policy, more generally, with the actual effect — perverse in terms of the government's objective — of reducing rather than enhancing their propensity to invest in the economy.

A corollary argument is that as competition among governments heats up, the negative effects can be expected to extend beyond the pressures to engage in bidding wars on fiscal and financial incentives. They can notably be expected to create strong downward pressures on effective public standards of protection (*de facto* and/or *de jure*) of the environment and of workers' rights. The concern over the environment is that governments will increase their willingness, to one degree or another, to become "pollution havens" in order to attract certain types of investment, notably in heavy industry. The concern over workers' rights is that whether or not governments actually change their labour legislation, they will become more lax about enforcing workers' rights to organise and bargain collectively, enforcing minimum job safety standards, etc.

These downward pressures on labour and environmental standards, it is argued, can even lead to a process of "regulatory arbitrage" as investors play governments off against one another in terms of local production costs. Such pressure — or governments' fear, or anticipation, of such pressure — can trigger a process of competitive downgrading of standards (the prisoner's dilemma) not unlike the destructive process of competitive currency devaluations that emerged in the 1930s. Such a process predictably would be neither constrained nor guided, moreover, by any government's concept of socially optimal levels of standards, anywhere.

Both bidding wars on incentives and downward pressures on standards or regulatory arbitrage are thus seen by the negative-sum game line of reasoning as the likely result of intensifying inter-governmental competition to attract FDI. While investors are seen as the immediate beneficiaries, at the expense of governments and host economies, in a longer-term perspective the inefficiencies, instabilities and rent-seeking behaviour to which these dynamics can be expected to give rise would suggest, ultimately, a significant net global loss. Hence the appropriateness of the "negative-sum game", as distinct from "zero-sum game", label for this interpretation of the effects of that competition.

Incentives-based and Rules-based Competition

The negative-sum game interpretation of the effects of policy competition among governments highlights a useful conceptual distinction between "incentives-based" and "rules-based" forms of competition. Incentives-based forms refer to fiscal and financial incentives. Common *fiscal* incentives include a reduction in the base income tax rate a particular category or categories of investors must pay (e.g. foreign investors, investors in certain types of activity); tax holidays (on income tax, on national or local sales taxes, on other taxes collected by national or sub-national governments); exemptions from import duties or duty drawbacks; accelerated depreciation allowances; investment and re-investment allowances; specific deductions from gross earnings for income-tax purposes; and deductions from social security contributions.

The most important *financial* incentives are grants; also widely used are subsidised loans and loan guarantees. These incentives are frequently targeted, at least nominally, for specific purposes, such as grants for labour training, wage subsidies, donations of land and/or site facilities, rebates on the cost of electricity and water, and loan guarantees for international lines of credit. Government provision or subsidisation of "dedicated" infrastructure (railroads, roads, industrial sites, sewage treatment facilities and the like built specifically for the investment project) is also common practice — with local, regional (e.g. state) and national governments often combining their financial "efforts" — and can be counted, for our purposes, as a type of financial incentive[4].

Both fiscal and financial incentives may be granted automatically (subject to qualifying conditions) or with up to a high degree of discretion by the administrative authority. (Discretion is often seen as a necessary condition for successful negotiation with investors, to ensure efficient targeting of incentives, and to allow for quick responses to competition. It also reduces transparency, of course, and increases the scope for abuse and corruption.) That authority may be at the level of local or municipal government, regional or state government (in a federal system), national government, or even at the supra-national level in the case of the European Union (whose Commission regulates the use of the "regional aids" which national and sub-national EU governments use to attract investors). Incentives can be granted conditionally or unconditionally, with conditional incentives sometimes linked to performance requirements — which call on the investor to attain certain levels of local-content in production, or exports, for example — in which case the incentives may be seen as "compensation" for the disincentive effect of the performance requirements.

Rules-based forms of competition are a broader and more heterogeneous group of government actions, ranging from changes in the rules on workers' rights or protection of the environment — or in the level of enforcement of existing rules — to the signing of regional-integration treaties with neighbouring countries, for example, as a means to attract FDI. Other important rules-based means which governments use to attract FDI include greater protection of intellectual property rights, strengthening the rule of law and improved judicial systems, the establishment of "export-processing zones" or "special economic zones" with distinct legislation from the rest of the country, the privatisation of state-owned enterprises, market deregulation, and, of course, the liberalisation of trade and investment policies.

The negative-sum game line of interpretation sees both incentives-based and rules-based forms of competition for FDI as having negative effects whose incidence is likely to be both economic and political. It posits that the economic cost of incentive bidding wars can be very high, in terms of the value of resources drained from the public treasury, but also in terms of the damage that can be done by market distortions and resource misallocation. The cost to the broader policy-making process within governments is also seen as likely to be high, not least because of the widespread *need* for lack of transparency in the use of incentives, and the consequent difficulty to control abuse and corruption that can be associated therewith. These effects are seen, moreover, as likely to be cumulative, self-reinforcing, and mutually reinforcing over time, with growing damage caused both to the body politic and to the economy.

The positive-sum game interpretation, on the other hand, sees both incentives-based and rules-based forms of competition as having positive effects. While it sees incentives-based competition bringing investment in both human-capital formation and infrastructure closer to socially optimal levels, for the mutual benefit of investors and economies, and sees it likely to increase the global supply of investment, again with significant net benefits for society as a whole, analogous reasoning leads it to point up significant additional potential benefits from rules-based competition. These include the considerable pressures on governments to create a more secure legal environment; to enhance the stability, transparency and credibility of economic policies in general, and perhaps (therefore) to help strengthen political stability, as well as to improve the quality of macroeconomic policies; to engage in regional integration schemes that help serve not only to increase the size but also the *contestability* of domestic markets, thereby favouring efficiency and dynamism and working against the accumulation of rigidities and damaging oligopolistic rent-seeking behaviour in those markets; and to protect intellectual property rights more effectively, which arguably promotes the inflow of advanced technologies and know-how. The intensification of competition among governments to attract FDI, and real investment as a whole, is thus seen by the positive-sum game interpretation as stimulating governments into behaving — or behaving more — in ways that favour the growth of investment, efficiency and productivity levels, and thus real income, in individual countries and globally. Investors and the economies of governments that compete for their investment are seen as benefiting substantially.

This Study

The chapters that follow address three related sets of questions to which the preceding debate gives rise.

The first set of questions concerns the *pattern* of competition to attract FDI: To what extent do governments — national, sub-national — actually compete with one another in seeking to attract real investment? Who competes with whom? (For example, do sub-national governments compete mostly with other sub-national governments? Do such governments compete mostly within national boundaries, or across national boundaries as well? Do national governments compete with sub-national governments? Do governments, at whatever level, compete mostly with their neighbours, or with others as well? Among which governments is the competition most active or intense?) Also, what are the principal *means* by which governments compete — and is there any significant evolution in those means? And, most importantly (looking to the future), to what extent is the competition among governments for FDI *intensifying*, or likely to intensify?

The second set of questions concerns the *effects* of the competition: What are its effects, and of its likely evolution? These effects may be thought of as consisting of three types: effects on investors' decisions *per se* (where to locate their investments, and how much to invest); effects on the broader economy (e.g. enhanced productivity levels due to the increased supplies of human capital and infrastructure induced by the competition for FDI, effects on regional income distribution within countries, effects on *de facto* labour standards); and effects on the broader policy-making process, beyond FDI policy *per se* (e.g. effects on government accountability and policy transparency, effects on governments' defence of labour and environmental standards, effects on policies toward regional integration among countries, effects on macroeconomic policy).

The third set of questions concerns the *implications for policy makers* of the answers to the previous two sets of questions. Of particular interest for our purposes are the implications for policy makers concerned with promoting economic and social development in developing and emerging economies, and those concerned with relations between those economies and OECD countries.

The first set of questions, and to a significant degree the second set as well, are of a kind that should lend themselves to empirical analysis. The great difficulty, however, is to obtain the necessary information. Neither investors nor governments readily provide that information. The analyses that follow are thus based on very incomplete information derived largely from a group of country reports undertaken in conjunction with this study. The reports are on Argentina, Brazil, Canada, the Caribbean Basin, China, Europe, India, Malaysia, Mexico, Singapore and the United States[5]. Much attention is given in those reports to the role of sub-national governments — states in the United States, Brazil, India and Mexico, provinces in Canada and China, regional and local governments in Europe — because it is those governments that turn out, in many cases, to be the most active players in the game of competing to attract FDI.

Chapter 2 examines *incentives-based* competition in six developing and emerging economies — Brazil, Argentina, Singapore, Malaysia, China and India — which together account for over half of FDI in all developing and emerging economies, and provides an overview of incentives-based competition in OECD countries (with a focus on the United States, Western Europe and Canada, whose experiences are also rich in lessons for developing and emerging economies). Chapter 3 then looks at *rules-based* competition, focusing on specific issues — the "pollution haven" and "labour standards" debates, and the role of regional-integration agreements, privatisation, and government accountability.

Chapter 4 concludes with a presentation of the study's findings and policy implications.

Notes

1. See also Oman (1996*a*).

2. See, for example, Weigel, Gregory and Wagle (1997) and Reuber *et al.* (1973). See also Ahmed and Root (1978) and Aharoni (1966).

3. See Aharoni (1966).

4. Governments can also seek to enhance their attractiveness to FDI through policies (including public investments) aimed at promoting the development of domestic infrastructure and other local "factors of production" (e.g. human skills) which may not be "dedicated" to a particular FDI project. For an analysis of policy competition that includes "factor creation" policies along with "incentives-based" and "rules-based" forms of policy competition, see Mortimore and Peres (1998).

5. Cf. Campos (1998), Da Motta Veiga and Iglesias (1998), A. Raynauld and F. Raynauld (1998), Chen (1998), Bachtler *et al.* (1998*)*, Venkatesan *et. al.* (1998) Sieh Lee (1998), Noyola and Espinosa (1998) Chia (1998), Donahue (1998) and Kuo and Chen (1998) — all reports prepared for the Development Centre. See also Mortimore and Peres (1998).

Chapter 2

Incentives-based Competition

Aggregate statistics on the fiscal and financial incentives that governments give to foreign direct investors are not available. A study whose empirical findings are therefore of considerable relevance for our purposes is the 1996 UNCTAD report on *Incentives and Foreign Direct Investment*[1]; those findings are summarised by way of introduction to this chapter. (The 1998 OECD Report on *Harmful Tax Competition* is also important, but only indirectly relevant for our purposes because it focuses exclusively on ways in which the tax base shifts in financial services and other such highly mobile activities. Our focus, in contrast, is on competition for foreign direct investment, which generally is less mobile and whose analysis requires consideration of other factors[2].) We then look at the evidence on incentives-based competition for FDI in specific countries. A first section examines such competition in six developing and emerging economies, which account for more than half the FDI hosted by all developing and emerging economies: Brazil, Argentina, Malaysia, Singapore, China and India (of the six, only India is not yet a major host to FDI). The next section provides an overview of incentives-based competition in OECD countries, looking at patterns in the United States, Western Europe and Canada. We conclude the chapter with a summary of the global pattern of incentives-based competition that emerge from this evidence.

The UNCTAD Report

Country-by-country survey information on the provision of investment incentives by national governments in 103 countries (OECD and non-OECD) during the period from the mid-1980s through to the early 1990s — information which Price Waterhouse, the Economics Intelligence Unit, Arthur Anderson and others collected and published in their periodical country reports on local economic and business conditions — is reported by UNCTAD as pointing to the following patterns and trends:

— Both the number of countries that offer incentives and the range of incentives they offer have grown considerably since the mid-1980s. Incentives competition among sub-national governments has also grown in many countries.

— Non-OECD governments appear to use fiscal incentives to a greater extent than financial incentives, whereas OECD governments appear to use financial incentives more than fiscal incentives. Reasons for this difference, according to UNCTAD, include *i)* while financial incentives tend to offer governments greater administrative flexibility than fiscal incentives, non-OECD governments tend more than OECD governments to lack the resources necessary to pay for direct financial incentives; and *ii)* in OECD countries, setting up fiscal incentive programmes often requires cumbersome parliamentary approval procedures. (The UNCTAD report, it should also be noted, focuses on the incentives given mainly by national governments, not on those offered by sub-national governments.)

— A few countries have made efforts to curtail fiscal incentives (e.g. Indonesia abolished tax holidays in 1984; Korea reduced both barriers and incentives to inward FDI) and some countries, e.g. Malaysia, have reduced the *relevance* of their fiscal incentives by reducing their base tax-rate for all firms. But such efforts are few in number and do not appear to have led to any significant curtailment of incentives competition as a whole (Indonesia even reintroduced tax holidays in 1997).

— The general pattern — and increasingly prevalent pattern as barriers to FDI come down — is for governments, in principle, not to differentiate between domestic and foreign investment in the design or implementation of incentives. There are, however, important exceptions (to be discussed later).

— A relatively large and growing proportion of countries target incentives to attract investment in specific types of activity or geographic areas. The principal targets, in descending order of frequency, are: *i)* specific *sectors*, notably high-tech and high-value-added manufacturing, for example in electronics and software, followed by modern *infrastructure*, and the *regional headquarters* of major corporations; *ii)* specific *regions* which are poorer or suffering from above-average unemployment, notably in Europe; *iii) exports*, notably in developing countries (the targeting of incentives to attract export-oriented investments has been reinforced by the Uruguay Round's TRIMs agreement because the latter curtails countries' ability to impose export performance requirements on investors); *iv) R&D, labour training*, and (especially in OECD countries) *job creation* or retention.

— Among *fiscal* incentives, the most widely used is a reduction in the base rate of corporate income tax. In OECD countries, the next most widely used, in descending order, are accelerated depreciation, specific deductions for corporate income-tax purposes, and reductions in other taxes (including state and local). In developing countries the next most widely used, after reduced base income-tax rates, are tax holidays, and import-duty exemptions and drawbacks[3].

— *Financial* incentives are widely used in OECD countries by sub-national governments and targeted to promote investment in specific regions or types of activity (and job creation or retention). In developing countries, they are less prominent than fiscal incentives but their use is growing.

The UNCTAD report thus concludes that competition for FDI with incentives is "pervasive" and even more intense in the 1990s than in the 1980s. It sees many governments increasing their incentives with the intention of diverting investment from competing jurisdictions, particularly on a regional (supra-national) basis. It argues that the growing use of incentives "involves substantial amounts of resources" and constitutes "a trend that is likely to continue". It also stresses the "lack of transparency in incentives practice" and the "widespread use of *ad hoc* incentives for major investment projects"[4].

As to the effects of this competition, the report states:

— While incentives are clearly a minor factor in investors' locational decisions (relative to the "fundamentals"), the impact of incentives is "not negligible". Their role becomes more important as other policy and non-policy variables converge across countries, especially for investment projects that are cost-oriented and mobile.

— Among targeted incentives, those geared to promoting exports have been most effective.

— Competition for FDI can have positive effects, as when it leads governments to refine their approach to investment promotion. Incentives can sometimes be justified to cover the gap between the social and private rates of return for FDI projects that create positive spillovers. Yet incentives also have the potential to introduce significant economic distortions (analogous to those caused by trade restrictions) as well as to impose significant public financial and administrative costs which are, moreover, very hard to measure.

— It is very difficult to determine whether any national welfare gains from competition come at the expense of other countries, or enhance world welfare. Clearly, in addition to the cost and waste imposed by incentives that exceed levels justified to cover the gap between the social and private returns on investment, and by distortions in the international allocation of investment, unbridled competition among governments for FDI "can lead to excesses as the world experienced in the inter-war period with successive rounds of currency devaluations in a beggar-thy-neighbour attempt to boost exports ..."[5].

— Within a country, one often finds conflict among the goals of an incentives programme, the actual design of the programme, and the capacity of the institutions charged with its administration. There is also generally a trade-off between targeted and more general incentives, with targeted incentives often increasing the potential impact but also the risk of distortions and biases that raise costs. Policy co-ordination among different levels of government is thus necessary to minimise incentives' undesirable side effects.

UNCTAD concludes that competition for FDI with incentives is "unlikely to be eliminated" but that excessive incentives can be "contained" and channelled into more effective areas, such as investment in public infrastructure. It believes unilateral action by a country can check the competitive behaviour of other countries to an extent. It calls for countries to undertake "a national FDI incentives review", and to ensure a proper balance between the use of incentives and investment *promotion* activities (the latter compete with incentives for the same scarce budget resources, are often more cost-effective at the margin, and tend less to fan the flames of cut-throat competition among governments).

UNCTAD also clearly calls for international co-operation to contain the excesses of incentives competition. It calls for "a step-by-step approach" to such co-operation "at the bilateral, regional and multilateral levels, which can be pursued simultaneously". It notes that some limited steps have been taken in this direction, notably: at the OECD; in the TRIMs (Trade-Related Investment Measures) and GATS (General Agreement on Trade in Services) Agreements signed in conjunction with the Uruguay Round of GATT/WTO multilateral trade negotiations; in some bilateral treaties (BITs, of which there are now some 1 600); within the European Union (the Commission controls state aids to regions and industries, often used to attract investors); and within the Caribbean Community (Caricom's 1973 Scheme for the Harmonisation of Fiscal Incentives to Industry) — and at the national level, in Canada, to contain incentives competition among sub-national jurisdictions (the Investment Chapter of the 1994 Agreement on Internal Trade). As UNCTAD also notes, and the Canadian experience is only one of many that are illustrative (see below), the task is made all the more difficult by the extent to which, in many countries, incentives competition is particularly fierce at the sub-national level.

Incentives-based Competition in Developing Countries

FDI inflows to developing countries rose from an annual average of $25 billion (17 per cent of global inflows) in 1985-90, to $149 billion (37 per cent of global inflows) in 1997. The share of global FDI that goes to these countries has thus more than doubled, and the volume has grown six-fold, over the last decade.

FDI flows to Latin America and the Caribbean rose from an annual average of $8 billion (33 per cent of developing-country inflows) in 1985-90, to $56 billion (38 per cent of developing-country inflows) in 1997. The combined share of Brazil and Argentina in the region's FDI inflows rose from 27 per cent in 1985-90, to 40 per cent in 1997 (Brazil's share rose from 16 to 29 per cent, Argentina's was a constant 11 per cent).

FDI flows to the developing Asian economies rose from an annual average of $13 billion (55 per cent of developing country inflows) in 1985-90, to $87 billion (58 per cent of developing country inflows) in 1997. The combined share of Malaysia, Singapore, China and India — the four Asian countries covered in this chapter — in developing Asia's FDI inflows rose from 51 per cent in 1985-90, to 72 per cent in 1997 (Malaysia's share fell from 8 to 4 per cent and Singapore's fell from 22 to 12 per cent, while China's share rose from 20 to 52 per cent and India's rose from 1 to 4 per cent).

Competition in Brazil[6]

Brazil has long been the largest host to FDI in Latin America, with a stock of some $126 billion as of end-1997 (among developing countries, only China hosts more FDI, with $217 billion at end-1997). The ratio of inward FDI stock to GDP in Brazil is about 14 per cent (as compared to about 16 per cent for all developing countries, and 8 per cent for OECD countries). FDI inflows, after stagnating from the mid-1980s through to 1993 at about $1.4 billion per year, on average, have grown significantly in recent years, to $5 billion in 1995, $11 billion in 1996 and over $16 billion in 1997[7].

Brazil was in fact the largest developing-country recipient of FDI from the 1950s until the second half of the 1980s (at which time Brazil's debt crisis and deteriorating macroeconomic situation caused investment to stagnate, including FDI, just as the flow of FDI into China accelerated[8]). From the 1950s to the 1980s, Brazil's federal government used relatively *dirigiste* industrial policy instruments — including major investments by state-owned enterprises and equity participation in joint ventures, as well as subsidised credits and fiscal incentives to promote private investment in specific sectors and regions — to pursue its strategy of import-substitution industrialisation. By developing-country standards, its treatment of FDI was liberal, its rules were stable, and the significant protection from imports it provided for its large and relatively fast-growing market served as a strong attraction to manufacturing FDI aimed at serving the domestic market.

The federal government thus exercised strong influence over the decisions, including the locational decisions, of both domestic and foreign corporate investors from the 1950s until the 1980s[9]. It also defined the objectives and controlled the mechanisms for implementing its regional development policies, which were designed to promote investment in the North, Centre-West and especially the Northeast — Brazil's poorest regions. It gave little consideration to competition for investment with other countries, and discouraged the modest attempts made by some of the country's state and municipal governments to compete directly to attract investment. At a time when political liberties were severely restricted, the latter type of competition occurred mainly through negotiations between state governors and the federal authorities.

Macroeconomic Deterioration and Institutional Change

The 1980s, however, witnessed a marked deterioration of Brazil's macroeconomic situation, notably after the eruption of the debt crisis in 1982. That deterioration, which continued until the "Real" stabilisation plan of July 1994, caused the gradual dissolution of the federal government's centralised mechanisms for the promotion of investment, along with that of both its national industrial policy (and strategy of deepening import-substitution industrialisation) and its regional-assistance policy. The macroeconomic deterioration also discouraged investment in production as a whole.

It was in this context of macroeconomic deterioration that there emerged in Brazil a process of decentralisation of fiscal powers, and resources, favouring the states (and, secondarily, municipal governments). That process combined with the building macroeconomic crisis to reverse the centralising fiscal reforms (notably those of the military regime in 1965), thereby also effectively dissolving Brazil's institutional controls on competition among sub-national governments for corporate investment[10]. The process was largely driven by the *political* desire for more democracy — supported by both the left and the economically liberal opposition to the military[11] — and was linked to the institutional strengthening of the legislative branch of the federal government, relative to the executive branch, as well as to the return to democracy. It culminated in the 1988 Constitution, which established the principle of fiscal federalism in Brazil, along with the imperative of reducing the severe disparities of income and living conditions between Brazil's poorest regions (the North, Northeast and Centre-West) and its richer regions (the South and Southeast) — disparities which only worsened during the 1980s.

Sub-national governments thus began to increase their spending significantly already during the latter half of the 1980s and early 1990s. Those expenditures grew particularly in the areas of public health, education and housing. Many states also designed incentive programmes to attract investment. Those programmes had little effect, however, because of the strong disincentive to invest caused by the deteriorating macroeconomic situation. As Da Motta Veiga and Iglesias note, "the space left by the Federal Government in the area of industrial promotion was not filled by sub-national governments during this period because there was little investment and thus little demand for incentives — not because sub-national governments were unprepared to offer incentives"[12].

Activation of Policy Competition

Policy competition to attract investment was "activated" in Brazil by the dramatic success of the 1994 "Real Plan" in cutting inflation and bringing macroeconomic stability to the country. One reason the Plan had this effect is that conditions favourable to investment in production — and investment planning — were finally restored, and both domestic and foreign investment responded accordingly. Another reason, perhaps less anticipated, was the distributional impact of the Plan in favour of the poorer segments of the population. That distributional impact has had both sectoral and regional dimensions: demand growth has been particularly strong for lower-income as well as middle-class consumer goods, both durable and non-durable; and demand growth in the poorest regions has been higher than the national average — highlighting the consumption potential of those markets[13].

Also important have been the consolidation of the "Mercosur" regional-integration process after December 1994, when agreement was reached with Argentina, Paraguay and Uruguay to achieve a Common Market, and Brazil's on-going unilateral policy and regulatory reforms to liberalise trade, investment and domestic competition. Average import tariffs fell from 32 per cent in 1990 to 14 per cent in 1994, for example, and privatisation of state-owned enterprises, notably in infrastructure (e.g. railroads, ports, utilities, telecommunications), has recently accounted for a quarter of all incoming FDI. All these policy changes and regulatory reforms are helping to attract FDI, as well as to promote domestic investment, which have grown rapidly since 1994. All are also thus helping to stimulate competition to attract investment in Brazil, which has indeed become very active since (and only since) 1994.

Trade liberalisation and regulatory reform combined with competition among sub-national governments to attract investment are having two types of effect on the location or relocation of production in Brazil. One effect, which Da Motta Veiga and Iglesias refer to as "restricted decentralisation", involves some movement away from Brazil's traditional industrial pole in São Paulo to other sites in the South and Southeast regions, i.e. to areas which are relatively wealthy and benefit from economies of agglomeration in technologically relatively sophisticated activities, such as automobiles and auto parts, electronics and telecommunications equipment. The Mercosur integration process and many of the country's regulatory reforms (the latter often cited by government officials as needed to attract FDI in modern services) also tend to promote this effect. The other effect is a relocation of some production away from the South and Southeast altogether — sometimes involving actual plant relocations — to sites in the North, Northeast and Centre-West, notably in such traditional labour-intensive consumer goods as clothing and footwear, along with food products, beverages, hygiene and cleaning products. Proximity both to export markets in the United States and Europe and to newly expanding consumer markets in Brazil's poorer regions, as well as lower labour costs, are important reasons for this relocation.

The Auto Regime

Particularly important as a stimulus to both these effects has also been the federal government's Auto Regime, launched in the wake of the 1995 Mexican crisis and Brazil's growing auto trade deficit, the latter caused by the explosion of domestic demand for cars due to reduced import tariffs and the currency appreciation that both followed the Plan. Officially justified as a means to attract investments in this sector needed to compensate for the auto regime Argentina launched in 1991 — which, it was feared, would divert to Argentina investment planned for the auto sector in the context of Mercosur — Brazil's auto regime is based on a significant new increase in import tariffs on automobiles (raised from 20 to 70 per cent, initially) combined with major tariff reductions on equipment, inputs and finished vehicles for companies that produce vehicles in Brazil, including for export. Additional incentives, mainly in the form of exemptions from federal taxation, are offered to firms that locate production in the North, Northeast and Centre-West. The auto regime is scheduled to terminate at the end of 1999 for investments in the South and Southeast, and in 2010 for investments in the North, Northeast and Centre-West.

Since 1995, there has been a literal explosion of investments, and investments announced, in the auto sector. The investors include General Motors, Ford, Chrysler, Renault, VW-Audi, Mercedes, Honda, Hyundai and several other producers of various types of motor vehicles. The combined value of their investment projects amounts to some $19 billion — of which about $2.7 billion (involving some 25 projects, mostly to produce commercial vehicles, motor cycles and tractors) is scheduled to be invested in the North, Northeast and Centre-West[14].

The "Fiscal War"

The auto regime has been accompanied by fierce competition among sub-national governments to attract investments in this sector. That competition lies at the heart of what has come to be called "the fiscal war" among the states in Brazil — and constitutes the core of incentives-based competition to attract investment in Brazil. (Thus, in Brazil as in many other countries, while sub-national governments that compete to attract corporate investment make no formal or legal distinction between the incentives they offer to foreign investors and those they offer to promote or attract domestic investment, in actual practice that competition tends to be heavily biased towards attracting FDI.)

A typical auto-sector investment incentives package offered by sub-national governments includes both financial and fiscal incentives, and both state and municipal governments commonly participate[15]. The value of the fiscal incentives (commonly state sales-tax holidays and exemptions from municipal taxes) tends, however, to be much larger than that of the financial incentives (which commonly include the provision and preparation of the project site and buildings, along with dedicated infrastructure). Unofficial figures derived mainly from press reports suggest, for example, that Volkswagen's investment project in the State of Rio de Janeiro, whose agreement was signed in July 1995 and was scheduled to create 1 800 direct jobs, benefited from financial incentives worth about $14 million (for dedicated infrastructure) and fiscal incentives worth between $83 and $155 million. The implied incentives cost per direct job, as shown at the end of this chapter in our table on *Investment Incentives in the Automobile Industry*, is thus between $54 000 and $94 000, of which fiscal incentives constitute between 86 and 92 per cent — a share that appears typical[16].

Comparable figures are available for Renault's investment project in Paraná, whose contract was signed in March 1996, and Mercedes' investment in Minas Gerais, signed in the second quarter of 1996. For the investment in Paraná, the figures suggest a total cost of incentives per direct job of about $133 000, of which fiscal incentives constitute 88 per cent. For the investment in Minas Gerais, the figures point to a total cost of incentives per direct job of about $340 000, of which 92 per cent are fiscal incentives[17].

While it would seem to be going a bit far to cite these figures as indicating a longer-term *intensification* of incentives competition for FDI in Brazil today, since active competition in the country is so recent, they certainly are compatible with the hypothesis of such an intensification. Da Motta Veiga and Iglesias point in particular, in this regard, to the fact that whereas in the case of the VW investment in Rio de Janeiro (which was one of the first projects signed following the creation of the Auto

Regime) the duration of the tax holiday is 5 years, that duration had already been lengthened to 30 years in the agreement between GM and Rio Grande do Sul less than two years later[18]. Also suggestive is the fact that because of its long-standing ability to attract FDI without offering incentives, the State of São Paulo for years actively opposed other states' attempts to offer incentives; but São Paulo recently caved in — because of intensifying competition? — and, in July 1996, introduced its own investment-incentives programme[19].

Da Motta Veiga and Iglesias further note that, overall, the major auto-sector investment projects announced and launched in Brazil since 1995 seem to have been decided by investors on the basis of global sectoral competitiveness criteria and the strong growth of demand in Brazil since 1993, combined with the country's new-found macroeconomic stability, independently of state-government incentives[20]. Moreover, the benefits the investors derive under the federal auto regime already provide them major savings on investment costs. "Why, then," ask the authors, "do state governments add subsidies to this already favourable situation for private investment[21]?" The answer, they assert, is that "incentive bidding wars are a reality" among sub-national governments today in Brazil[22].

The Broader Context

Looking beyond the auto industry *per se*, however, to the phenomenon of the relocation of production in some industries from the wealthier southern regions to the poorer northern regions, the authors also highlight the growing mobility and readiness of firms to relocate within the country. In that context, they cite investor survey results which identify fiscal incentives and market proximity as the two most important factors, followed by labour costs, in explaining the relocation phenomenon[23]. This evidence would seem to suggest not only that incentives are playing a key role in many investment-location decisions in Brazil, but that incentives-based competition in Brazil may well remain strong, or even intensify, in the coming years.

While incentives-based competition is most intense at the level of state governments, and secondarily at the level of municipalities (whose governments often team up with their state government to compete against sites in other states), the federal government is responsible for the auto regime and, as such, responsible for Brazil's most significant and elaborate investment-incentives scheme. That scheme reproduces an industrial-policy approach typical of import-substitution industrialisation, characterised by strong sectoral discrimination which effectively penalises other sectors (notably including auto parts in this case). The scheme is reproduced, and its effects greatly amplified, by state governments' competition to attract investments in this sector.

The federal government is additionally responsible for incentives-based competition in Brazil today in the sense that it has avoided any attempt to limit such competition among the states and municipalities. This is true, first, because the federal government has consistently failed to apply existing legislation (notably a 1975 law) which authorises it to impose limits. It is true, secondly, because the country's president and the legislative leadership of states in the poorer regions have agreed to block a recent initiative of the federal Senate to limit the states' use of investment incentives. The poorer regions' desire to use incentives to compete with the wealthier states to attract FDI thus appears to be supported by the president, and, in addition to the announced concern over possible investment diversion to Argentina, may also be an important factor behind the auto regime.

There is, in any case, broad agreement in Brazil that the loss of the federal government's efficiency in regional-development policy is a major driving force behind the "fiscal war" among the states. In Brazil as in other countries, there is thus an important, if somewhat less than transparent, relationship between the executive authority's use of investment incentives (and its allowance of states to use incentives) and its desire to promote development in the poorer regions by inducing investment in those regions. In Brazil, more specifically, the activation of incentives-based competition since 1994 marks the culmination of a process of dissolution, underway since the mid-1980s, of the country's relatively *dirigiste* import-substitution industrialisation development strategy. That dissolution is accompanied by a process of policy decentralisation in which fiscal resources and responsibilities are transferred from the federal government to the states (and secondarily to municipalities). This process of fiscal federalism, which is also closely linked to the process of political democratisation in Brazil, has led to growing involvement by sub-national governments in the design and implementation of social policies from the early 1990s. More recently, i.e. since the 1994 activation of incentives-based competition to attract investment, it has started to involve sub-national governments in the design and implementation of "industrial" policies — or what might also be called "competitiveness" policies.

This decentralisation process is also occurring in a broader context of regulatory reform, regional integration (Mercosur), privatisation, and trade and investment liberalisation (with the notable exception of the auto regime), all of which tend to strengthen market forces and contribute to the modernisation of the public sector. Increasingly, in other words, the logic of investment-location decisions is essentially a private one governed by cost and competitiveness criteria, rather than by political negotiations between (unelected) state and federal officials as was the case previously.

This new, emerging, context also induces sub-national governments increasingly to modernise and organise themselves more flexibly with a view to enhancing local competitiveness. They are learning not only how to negotiate incentives but to help investors identify investment opportunities, target potential investors, co-ordinate and professionalise their actions, and improve their own learning skills.

It would thus be wrong to dismiss the "fiscal war" or incentives-based competition in Brazil today as mere fiscal irresponsibility on the part of sub-national governments in the current context of policy decentralisation and fiscal federalism. That competition, which is so new in Brazil, is part of a larger process of transition away from the *dirigiste* regime of the post-war era to the much more open, democratic, and market-friendly regime that is now in the making[24].

Negative Effects

The negative effects of incentives-based competition in Brazil today cannot be ignored. One is, of course, the fiscal impact: though difficult to quantify, the long-term nature of the tax incentives widely provided by sub-national governments means that the impact on those governments' fiscal balances will be both large and long-lasting. Perhaps even more worrisome are the effects likely to stem from the strongly discriminatory nature of the auto regime. The relationship of dependence, both economic and political, which the auto regime establishes between governments and industry — typical of those prevailing under import-substitution industrialisation — can be expected to stimulate both protectionist demands and rent-seeking behaviour in the industry. Significant overcapacity, a bias against small firms, and an anti-export bias are further likely consequences of the market distortions the auto regime introduces.

One could add to this list of negative effects the increased potential for conflict with neighbouring countries especially in the context of Mercosur, notably with Argentina, and the damage such conflict could do to the regional-integration process. That risk has already led Argentina to advance proposals for greater harmonisation of rules on sub-national governments' use of fiscal incentives in the two countries or the adoption of a single incentives regime for Mercosur's poorer regions. Da Motta Veiga and Iglesias thus speculate that incentives-based competition for investment among the states in Brazil "may come to be revealed as an indispensable prerequisite for Mercosur's members to accept to undertake negotiations on which policy instruments to attract investment should be permitted, actionable, and prohibited, under the rules of Mercosur"[25].

On the issue of market distortions, Da Motta Veiga and Iglesias also note, reassuringly, that the site-location choices for investment projects tend to be made "as if investors selected the states [of their investment sites] that present the lowest political and economic risk of suspending the incentives"[26]. The main factor distinguishing states that tend to be successful in attracting investors from those that do not, they further note, is not whether a state is poor or rich, or in a particular region, but whether its strategy to attract investors is, or is not, part of a broader process of mobilisation within the state around a "project of social and political change ... in which the government redefines its role and its relationship with society and, in particular, with the traditional elites and local vested interests consolidated during the period of import-substituting industrialisation"[27].

The Future

Looking to the future, Da Motta Veiga and Iglesias thus conclude that the central policy challenge will be to find the best way to manage incentives-based competition among sub-national governments, rather than to try to suppress it or to allow what can easily become predatory competition. Taking a relatively positive view of the dynamics of competition, they claim that "it is not by chance that some of the states that are most successful in [competing to attract investment] are exactly those where the requirements for good government seem to be met, and where the state's good financial situation provides legitimacy ... to the concession of fiscal incentives without excessive costs for public finances: the state government's capacity over time to maintain its fiscal obligations seems to be working as an important — and healthy — variable in policy competition"[28].

The authors' optimism is only bolstered, finally, by the growing exposure of firms in Brazil, foreign and domestic, to international competition. That exposure reduces the risk of serious allocational distortions caused by incentives competition both in the auto industry — where the bulk of new capacity actually will be located in sites which the authors describe as "a natural extension" of the existing auto complex — and in the labour-intensive sectors such as footwear that are relocating to the northern regions where, according to the authors, "incentives seem only to have accelerated a structural tendency for relocation in pursuit of lower production costs, and could also be contributing to the ... reconversion of depressed or very poor regions"[29].

With the auto regime terminating at the end of 1999, the authors recommend a federal policy towards the auto sector that eliminates or minimises factors that stimulate rent-seeking behaviour (such as quotas), is in conformity with WTO rules, and is less discriminatory against auto parts. At the sub-national level, they recommend the establishment of obligatory disclosure of information needed to monitor the use of incentives, and the introduction of criteria to discipline their use. These criteria could also promote sub-national governments' development of competitiveness policies through alternative means which also help reduce income disparities within and among states.

To these recommendations one could add two further suggestions: encourage a shift from fiscal to financial incentives, particularly insofar as the latter are used to produce infrastructure with significant "public good" attributes. And encourage a shift from incentives-based competition towards greater emphasis on rules-based competition in Brazil.

Competition in Argentina[30]

With an inward FDI stock about one-quarter the size of Brazil's ($36 billion at end-1997, as compared to $126 billion in Brazil), Argentina is the third largest host to FDI in Latin America, after Mexico ($87 billion). Argentina's ratio of FDI stock to GDP, at about 10 per cent, is below the regional average (Brazil's ratio is 14 per cent, and those for South America and for Latin America and the Caribbean as a whole are, respectively, 14 and 17 per cent). FDI inflows have grown strongly in Argentina in the 1990s, from an annual average of barely $500 million in the 1980s to $4.8 billion by 1995, $5 billion in 1996 and over $6 billion in 1997[31].

Argentina is nevertheless similar to Brazil in a number of important respects. Both countries pursued import-substitution strategies of industrialisation during the post-war period, characterised by relatively *dirigiste* industrial policies and predominantly undemocratic political regimes, which largely "dissolved" in conjunction with the severe debt crisis of the 1980s. Both returned to democratic political regimes in the 1980s, and, after suffering from prolonged high inflation, both launched successful far-reaching macroeconomic stabilisation programmes in the 1990s — Argentina in April 1991[32], Brazil in July 1994. Together, the two countries are the driving force of the Mercosur regional integration process. Both have moved strongly in recent years, and continue to move, towards more market-friendly economic policy regimes — including major regulatory reform, privatisation, and liberalisation of trade and investment policies — while introducing a highly discriminatory policy regime in the automobile industry.

A major difference between the two countries, however, is that, whereas in Brazil there has been a process of decentralisation of fiscal resources and responsibilities from the federal government to the states and, secondarily, to municipalities, in Argentina the provinces have not benefited from such a process of fiscal federalism. Argentina's provincial governments are thus not in a position to offer major fiscal incentives to attract investors, and their financial constraints prevent them from offering major financial incentives as well[33]. Only in the latter half of the 1990s have some provinces begun more actively to compete to attract investors, mainly via promotion campaigns both within the country and abroad (with some provinces putting their relatively sound fiscal and financial situation at the centre of their advertising campaign to attract investors).

Incentives-based competition among sub-national governments in Argentina is thus relatively insignificant. Much more important is the role of rules-based competition, a subject to which we return in Chapter 3. Argentina does, however, have two major sector-specific policy regimes to attract FDI which deserve comment.

Mining Regime

One is in mining, a sector which for many years "benefited" from major fiscal incentives in the form of a 7-year exemption from the country's value-added tax, followed by an additional 8 years of major reductions in that tax. These incentives were part of an investment-incentives regime that favoured projects aimed at the domestic market and gave state-owned firms the "upper hand" in major investment decisions. They cost an estimated $500 million in foregone tax revenues between 1975 and 1996, during a period when production in the sector declined in many years. That incentives regime culminated in 1992, on the eve of the new mining regime, with annual investment in mining production averaging only about $10 million, and mining exports amounting to only $16 million. Referring to that period, many firms report "bad memories of the numerous [times when] different fiscal packages were introduced" which created considerable fiscal instability and made it difficult to plan investments — in a sector where projects typically require many years from the time major investments must be made in exploration and site development until pay-back levels of output can be attained[34].

Those fiscal incentives were eliminated in 1993, when the new mining regime was launched. Since then, the value of annual investment in mining production has risen to $564 million in 1997, and that of exports to an estimated $700 million in 1998, while some 7 000 jobs have been created in construction and infrastructure projects at several mine sites — many of them in relatively remote regions of the country with few employment alternatives[35]. Equally important, the number of foreign firms engaged in mining *exploration* — necessary for future production — has risen from only four in 1992 to no less than 80 in 1997, plus eight domestic firms.

An important reason for the success of the new mining regime is the financial stability and predictability it provides for investors, in the form of a 30-year guarantee of no federal tax increase. The new regime nevertheless eliminates the value-added tax exemption and reductions, and even introduces a small new tax in the form of a 3 per cent (maximum) royalty on production payable to the provincial government where a mine is located.

The decision to offer the 30-year guarantee of no tax increase reflects an important element of policy competition, notably with Chile (which offers a similar guarantee), as well as the government's recognition of the particular importance of tax stability in this sector. The new mining regime nevertheless avoids unbridled incentives-based competition, both because of its elimination of the costly value-added tax incentives of the previous regime and its introduction of a (modest) new tax, and because of the emphasis it puts on tax *stability*. Moreover, because it has already attracted enough new mining FDI to generate an estimated 15-year fiscal *surplus* in mining of about $650 million. To this fiscal success must be added the new regime's remarkable success in increasing the level of investment in exploration, the size of exports, and the amount of job creation — notably in some of the country's poorest regions. While one cannot totally disregard the risk that in creating a new source of royalty income the new regime may eventually stimulate some incentives-based competition among the provincial governments to which that royalty is payable, that risk seems small — not least because mining investment-location decisions depend heavily on the location of mineral lodes and are therefore less mobile than investments in other sectors, and because the maximum royalty is limited to a small share of the value of any investment project[36].

Auto Regime

The other major sector-specific policy regime in Argentina today is the auto regime. Established in the same year as the macroeconomic stabilisation plan (1991), it represents a significant change from the previous import-substitution regime particularly in the extent to which it opens the country's auto industry to external competition. It also encourages automakers producing in the country: *i)* to offset the value of their imports with exports (imports can include finished vehicles, on which firms producing in the country are given a highly preferential tariff rate, of 2 per cent, which is not given to firms that do not produce vehicles in the country); *ii)* to commit to a minimum level of investment; *iii)* to reduce the number of models they produce in the country (a number that has fallen from 25 in 1990 to 12 in 1997); and *iv)* to produce models recently introduced in the automakers' home countries.

Auto production has grown in Argentina from 100 000 units in 1991 to 470 000 units in 1997, exports have grown from 500 units to 270 000 units (of which 95 per cent go to Brazil) and the stock of recent investment in the industry is expected to reach $5.5 billion by the year 2000 — of which almost half by firms that were not producing vehicles in Argentina when the auto regime was launched (including GM, Toyota, Fiat and Chrysler). Manufacturing productivity levels have also doubled, as the auto regime's encouragement of specialisation and balanced trade in vehicles with Brazil has led to larger scales of production, significant cost reduction and the introduction of flexible post-taylorist "lean" methods of work organisation[37].

The success of Argentina's macroeconomic stabilisation programme has been important for the success of the new auto regime. Even more important however, according to interviews with auto-sector executives, has been the role of Mercosur — combined with the major OECD-based automakers' desire to be a part of large "emerging" middle-income markets with major growth potential — along with the sectoral discrimination of the auto regime[38]. Without Mercosur, according to investor surveys, the auto regime alone — even given the success of the stabilisation programme — would probably have been much less successful. Indeed, the credibility of Argentina's auto regime benefited greatly when in 1994 Mercosur's governing body recognised the validity of the regime, at least through 1999, along with the "domestic origin" status of Brazilian-produced auto components within the framework of Mercosur.

The major OECD-based auto companies have understood the "national" importance both Argentina and Brazil attach to their auto industries, and therefore that total free trade will not be allowed in the sector within Mercosur insofar as such trade could significantly shift the balance of auto production for the regional market in favour of either country to the detriment of the other. The auto companies reportedly see Mercosur as providing a good framework for achieving both stability and growth for the sector within the region, for several reasons: *i)* Mercosur usefully balances Argentina's current preference for a more open regional market (helpful for the companies to develop strong links with other parts of their international production networks) against Brazil's inclination towards ensuring a strong domestic industry (helpful for the established producers to preserve their regional dominance *vis-à-vis* outsiders); *ii)* Mercosur is more likely than are autonomous national auto regimes, particularly *vis-à-vis* the WTO, to be able to preserve a discriminatory sectoral regime that gives established producers some protection without putting them at a procurement-cost disadvantage *vis-à-vis* outsider firms; and *iii)* the established producers know that as in the case of NAFTA, future negotiations toward an hemispheric Free Trade Agreement of the Americas will include negotiations on rules of origin, for which they prefer there to be a united Mercosur position.

There are, however, tensions between Argentina and Brazil, along with co-operation between the two countries, over the auto industry in the context of Mercosur. Argentina is particularly sensitive to any policy changes that reduce auto producers' perceptions of the long-term *stability* of the regional "rules of the game" because of the tendency of any such changes to induce those companies to favour investment in Brazil's much larger market — which is four times the size of Argentina's — rather than take full advantage of Argentina's competitive advantages in production to serve the regional market. This concern for preserving stable rules within Mercosur is reflected in Argentina's proposals for a common set of rules on incentives-based competition to promote investment in poorer areas throughout Mercosur, and/or for harmonisation of rules on sub-national governments' use of fiscal incentives, mentioned earlier. It was after Brazil launched its own auto regime, with special provisions to promote investments in Brazil's poorer regions, that Argentina put forward these proposals.

Notwithstanding the sectoral discrimination involved in Argentina's auto regime, the country's overall policy-approach to attracting FDI since 1991 is, in sum, very much a "rules-based" rather than an "incentives-based" approach. As Campos notes, "the government has been preaching the benefits of an increasingly simplified market-driven economy as the best way to attract FDI". That policy orientation has been reinforced by "a broad consensus" in Argentina that the largely incentives-based approach to attracting FDI which prevailed in the 1970s and 1980s has a "bad reputation", due both to its lack of efficacy and to its lack of transparency[39]. Budget constraints imposed on the national government by the stabilisation programme reinforce that policy orientation.

This orientation is also reflected in the major role of the privatisation of state-owned enterprises in attracting FDI to Argentina: some 70 per cent of Argentina's FDI inflows since 1990 have been to purchase or invest in privatised firms, notably in such public utilities as electric power, gas and telephones. An important incentive for international banks to participate in these investments has been the possibility to convert debt into equity in privatised firms. Also reportedly important are regulations that in some cases have preserved the monopoly character of the privatised utility[40] — an issue to which we turn in Chapter 3.

The activation of incentives-based competition among states in Brazil since 1994 has also led to some recent questioning in Argentina of the wisdom of relying so heavily on "rules-based" means to attract FDI, and to growing perceptions among provincial governments in Argentina of the need to be active in seeking to attract FDI. Still, the signs are that any increased use of direct incentives to promote investment will be geared to helping small and medium-size firms, and to promoting investment in such relatively high-risk and slow-payback activities with significant potential positive spillover effects as, for example, forestry[41]. They also point to a broad consensus in Argentina on the need for public investment in education, in infrastructure, and in improving the judiciary in order to sustain and strengthen the country's attractiveness to domestic and foreign direct investors[42].

Competition in Malaysia[43]

From the time of its independence in 1957, Malaysia has given FDI a central role in the development of the nation's economy. That importance is reflected in the country's high ratio of inward FDI stock to GDP: at 49 per cent, the ratio is second only to Singapore's phenomenal 72 per cent, about twice Indonesia's 25 per cent, and several times those of Thailand (12 per cent), the Philippines (10 per cent) and developing Asia as a whole (15 per cent). FDI flows to Malaysia have risen from an annual average of about $1 billion in 1985-90, to a relatively stable yearly average of $4.6 billion in 1991-96 and $3.8 billion in 1997 (the 1997 figure reflecting the crisis that emerged in Asia that year)[44].

Three periods can be distinguished in the evolution of Malaysia's policy toward FDI. The first, from 1957 to 1968, corresponds to the import-substitution industrialisation period. Import barriers and fiscal incentives were used during this period, relatively successfully, to attract manufacturing FDI oriented mainly towards producing consumer goods for the domestic market.

The second period, from 1968 to 1982, witnessed policies that gave more emphasis to attracting export-oriented manufacturing FDI. Marked by the introduction of the Investment Incentives Act of 1968, this period saw substantial fiscal incentives offered especially to attract FDI in industries that were new to the country (notably electronics), to promote job creation (Malaysia was promoted as a low-cost production centre with abundant inexpensive trainable labour), and to encourage investment in less developed areas within the country.

The second period was also characterised by the rapid growth of "free trade zones", i.e. tax-free export-processing zones (see also Chapter 3 below) which allow foreign manufacturers to employ Malaysian workers — in practice, mostly young female workers — who are attracted from areas around the designated zones. It was during this period, following the 1969 "race riots", that the "New Economic Policy" was introduced as well. That policy, which lasted until 1990, sought to promote the economic interests of the native Malay or *bumiputra* population by limiting to 30 per cent the share of a firm's equity that could be foreign owned, and to 40 per cent the share that could be owned by Chinese (or other non-Malay) Malaysians — effectively promoting a strategy of minority-foreign-owned joint ventures[45].

The spread of "free trade zones" and similar "export platform" industrialisation strategies in other developing countries during this same period led to some competitive bidding and "more and more concessions" by Malaysia to attract competitive export-oriented FDI[46]. These fiscal incentives were accompanied by increasing attempts in Malaysia "to provide the most conducive investment environment through means that ensured a strong and growing economy, political stability, an educated and trouble-free workforce, adequate infrastructure and facilities for foreign investors, and minimum bureaucratic hassles"[47]. While policy towards FDI under the New Economic Policy was in fact relatively liberal — other than on the matter of equity ownership — the government felt it had to offer significant fiscal incentives to resolve "the dilemma of beckoning with one hand to much needed FDI ... while restraining, with the other hand, the share of foreign equity ... "[48].

The third period, which began in 1982 and continues today, can be described as "an integrated take-off phase ... in which trade and investment reinforce each other" and manufacturing FDI plays a central role in promoting trade in *intermediate* goods and services, as "sections of the same value chain [in production] increasingly are spread across different [national] economies"[49]. The current policy orientation is the consequence of several factors, including a marked economic slowdown in Malaysia in the mid-1980s which induced the government to relax constraints on foreign equity ownership from 1985 to 1990, and the post-Plaza Accord appreciation of the yen which stimulated substantial relocation of production capabilities to Malaysia, notably in electronics, by both Japanese and Chinese Taipei components and final-goods producers. The result was a significant surge of FDI inflows from the late 1980s until 1996, which contributed decisively to Malaysia's sustained 9 per cent average annual GDP growth during those years, along with strong export growth. That surge of FDI contributed to even stronger import growth, however, and thus to a trade deficit and growing current account deficits in the years leading up to the emergence of the crisis in Malaysia 1997[50].

Malaysia's policies toward FDI in this third period recognise, more fully than in the previous periods, both the need for some foreign affiliates to be able to import intermediate goods and services — because they may not be produced locally, or because local substitutes may not meet quality standards required for competition on global markets — and the need for some FDI in Malaysia to service the domestic market even if its output is mainly exported. The top policy priority is to promote increasingly high-tech or knowledge-intensive production that will be competitive on tomorrow's global markets. The principal means to attain this goal are policies to promote: the "integrated development of manufacturing cum services along value-added chains using a cluster approach"; the growing application of information technologies (notably in conjunction with development of the Multimedia Super Corridor[51]) along with an emphasis on training and skill development; and targeting efforts to attract major corporations' regional headquarters and international procurement centres[52].

Trends

Liberal fiscal incentives were officially introduced by the 1968 Investment Incentives Act, which also launched the policy shift toward attracting export-oriented manufacturing FDI. The incentives include tax holidays for "Pioneer Status" firms, investment tax credits, and tax relief for job creation and for firms that locate production in less developed parts of the country. The basic logic of granting fiscal incentives has not changed since then, although recent extensions have been made to provide incentives to attract investment in certain infrastructure or service activities, such as highly capital-intensive telecommunications projects and large convention and resort facilities.

Industry-specific fiscal incentives are offered and, overall, incentives increase with the priority of the activity or industry, with the size of the project, with the share of output to be exported, and with the share of equity owned by Malaysians.

The Promotion of Investment Act of 1986, amended in 1991, also provides incentives to encourage both local and foreign investors to invest in capital- and technology-intensive projects, and offers important fiscal incentives to FDI to strengthen domestic industrial linkages, to develop computer and information-technology assets, to invest in R&D, to promote worker training, to promote tourism, to invest in infrastructure, and to promote smaller firms, among others.

Tariff protection and import restrictions are also granted to certain industries "as temporary measures to prevent massive speculation that may upset the initial start-up phase of an industrial project, or to protect local production", while another important incentive that benefits most FDI is the exemption of most machinery and equipment required for an investment project but not produced locally from import duties, surtaxes and sales taxes. As Sieh notes, "Even without data on the cost of these measures to the Government, it is not difficult to visualise the immensity of the revenue foregone, simply because the economy is almost entirely dependent on foreign-made machinery and equipment. ... Fortunately, the economy has grown past the stage of [the Government's] relying heavily on tariff and border duties for revenue"[53].

Using data for 1996, Sieh offers the very rough estimate of about $2.4 billion in foregone surtax and sales tax revenues alone. Given that total manufacturing investment in Malaysia that year was about $13.7 billion, and that FDI accounted for about half that value and supplied somewhat less than half the 91 000 jobs created by that investment, one can infer that the revenue cost of those incentives, alone, was on the order of $30 000 per job created by FDI. While data on the cost to the government of the other fiscal incentives — notably the multi-year income-tax holidays and investment tax credits — are unavailable, that cost must be substantial.

The evidence does not, however, point to an *escalation* of the cost of fiscal incentives, relative to the size of FDI inflows, over time. Data for 1985 and 1996 on the proportion of approved manufacturing investment projects that received fiscal incentives show, on the contrary, some decline in that proportion. In 1985, 37 per cent of all projects received pioneer status or investment tax allowances, and those projects represented 74 per cent of the total value of approved investment and 58 per cent of the number of jobs to be created by all approved projects that year. By 1996, the proportion of approved projects receiving those fiscal incentives had declined to 28 per cent, representing 58 per cent of the value of total approved investment and 37 per cent of the jobs to be created that year[54].

Also noteworthy is the virtual absence, by international comparison, of incentives-based competition among the 13 state governments in Malaysia. Every state has its own Economic Planning Unit and State Economic Development Corporation, but, as Sieh observes, most states are not large geographically, and free and rapid movements between them has tended to diminish the importance of inter-state competition especially since the late 1980s, "because opportunities [to attract investment] have been abundant with very high GDP growth" in the country as a whole[55]. She adds that given "the political dominance of the ruling Barisan Nasional in all states but one, relations between the Federal Government and state governments have always been well co-ordinated, consistent and synchronised in most areas of economic policy and strategy"[56]. Most important of all, perhaps, is the fact that no state taxation system exists for corporate or personal income. The only direct sub-national sources of fiscal revenue are minor local licenses and fees, town council assessments levied for local services, and local land quit rent.

Differences nevertheless exist among the states, and land and related resources such as water are under the jurisdiction of state governments. As the national economy develops, the more developed states along the west coast of Peninsular Malaysia are expected to become congested, and competition in land-use management and redevelopment is likely to become more important as investors' attention turns more often to the east coast states in Peninsular Malaysia and Sarawak in East Malaysia. Inter-state competition may intensify through such financial incentives as the supply of investment sites, site preparation and related infrastructure[57].

Implications

There can be little doubt that Malaysia's long-standing and relatively intensive use of fiscal incentives, combined with its political stability and sound macroeconomic policies, has been an important contributor to the country's considerable success since the 1970s in attracting manufacturing FDI to serve international markets, notably in electronics. Nor can there be much doubt that the prevalence of industry-specific incentives has implied important distortions whose effects are difficult to gauge. Arguably, they have played an indirect role in generating the current account deficits of the 1990s that made the economy vulnerable to the events that produced the crisis in 1997; but the country's long-standing use of incentives, and the lack of evidence of any particular intensification of that use in the years preceding the crisis render such reasoning tenuous.

While the crisis itself can be expected to heighten competition among Asian developing countries to attract FDI, Malaysia was already facing growing competition, notably from the new Indochinese members of ASEAN, and from China. An important response to that (pre-crisis) growth of competition has been to promote the creation of an ASEAN Investment Area (AIA) as a valuable complement to the 1992 ASEAN Free Trade Agreement (AFTA). Although the details of AIA are still under discussion — and the use of regional-integration schemes to attract FDI is a subject to which we will return in Chapter 3 — it is important to note here that there is considerable ambivalence today about the likely benefits of AIA. On the one hand, the idea behind AIA is that greater co-operation among the ASEAN countries will lead to less competition among them because outsiders are more likely to approach the ASEAN region as a whole; combined with AFTA, it should enable multinational firms to pursue a division of labour within the region by facilitating their exploitation of the comparative advantages of various production sites selected for different parts of a production network or value chain spread across the region. The new Indochinese members are expected to have comparative advantages in unskilled labour-intensive products, and are accepted into ASEAN with the acknowledgement that they will divert some trade and investment from the older members, while the latter — especially Singapore and Malaysia — are expected to have comparative advantages in higher-skill-intensive goods and services. On the other hand, however, in the wake of the current crisis, member countries are reportedly rethinking the wisdom of projecting a single ASEAN image, especially when trying to counteract the contagion effect. These doubts are only amplified by new concerns about how soon the region's potentially powerful consumer market — in principle another strong inducement for investors to approach the region as a whole — will emerge in the wake of the crisis.

There are times, in other words, when highlighting *differences* among neighbours may be important. The implication, Sieh concludes, is that "both regional strategies and national programmes are needed ... the former for co-operative or joint efforts especially in negotiations where strength can be drawn from unity, the latter for competitive action when comparative advantages need to be stressed. Promotional work for FDI at both levels, though costly, will continue to be important"[58].

Competition in Singapore[59]

FDI has played a critical role in Singapore's economic development since before the country's independence in 1965. In power since independence, the People's Action Party (basically a labour party) has consistently centred the country's highly successful export-oriented industrialisation strategy on attracting FDI. The importance of FDI in Singapore is reflected in the country's ratio of inward FDI stock to GDP: at 72 per cent, the ratio is the highest in the world[60]. That importance is also reflected in the fact that 90 per cent of value added in Singapore's electronics industry (the industry whose development has driven Singapore's remarkable growth of exports and income over the last three decades) is accounted for by foreign investors, and that FDI accounts for fully two-thirds of equity capital in the country's manufacturing sector[61]. Indeed, with less than 1 per cent of the nine ASEAN countries' combined population, Singapore hosts a third of their combined inward FDI stock. FDI flows to Singapore have grown from an annual average of $3 billion in 1985-90 and $4.3 billion in 1991-94, to $8 billion in 1995, $9 billion in 1996 and $10 billion in 1997 — about 40 per cent of the ASEAN countries' combined FDI inflows in 1997[62].

In the early 1960s and following independence, Singapore's government felt it could not count on local capital and entrepreneurship to industrialise the economy — and thus create the jobs needed to absorb the economy's sizeable and growing unemployment — not only because they were in short supply, but because they were steeped in the traditions of entrepot and retail trade and had no experience in manufacturing for international markets. Moreover, unlike Korea and Chinese Taipei, where early industrialisation depended on import substitution, Singapore did not have a domestic market potentially large enough to absorb the learning costs of infant manufacturing firms and industries. Nor was Singapore able to spearhead its transition from entrepot trade to industrialisation with the influx of business people fleeing communism in China, who brought both capital and know-how, as Hong Kong did in the 1950s. Nor, finally, did Singapore have the bargaining leverage of either a large domestic market or abundant natural resources to enable its government bureaucrats or local capitalists to try to unbundle the FDI package and secure capital, technology and foreign expertise separately, via "new forms" of investment[63].

From the outset, then, Singapore's government turned to FDI as the key to enabling the economy to industrialise quickly and effectively, thereby creating jobs and raising long-term living standards. The financial inflow that came with FDI in those early years also helped to close the gap between investment and domestic savings, to finance net imports, and to cover the current account deficit[64].

By the 1980s, Singapore's GDP and export capabilities had grown significantly, and raised wage and income levels substantially. Domestic savings had risen to over 40 per cent of GDP, exceeding the rate of investment and thus reducing the financial need for FDI as Singapore became a net exporter of capital[65]. Yet the economy's reliance on inward FDI has not diminished. Private local enterprises remain relatively weak, and the economy continues to rely on FDI for entrepreneurship, management capabilities, technology, and marketing networks. Moreover, because foreign direct investors' profits and outward remittances have tended to move in close tandem with the general performance of Singapore's economy and the health of its balance of payments, while the economic risk-taking function is also borne by those investors, time and again Singapore's exceptional reliance on FDI has effectively cushioned its economy from the balance-of-payments and debt crises that have hurt many other developing economies. Since 1988, Singapore's current account has even registered a strong and growing surplus, reflecting the country's very high domestic savings rate (49 per cent of GNP, as compared to an investment rate of 35 per cent in 1995). This surplus, which averaged over $13 billion per year in 1994-96, combined with high capital inflows, has allowed Singapore's international reserves and outward investment to increase steadily[66]. It has also helped, insofar as possible, to shield Singapore from the current crisis that so many of Singapore's neighbours face.

Trends

To attract the highly competitive export-oriented manufacturing FDI that Singapore has sought since the early 1960s (FDI which tends to be considerably more footloose than both natural-resource-seeking and import-substitution manufacturing FDI) and to enable that investment right from its infancy, in Singapore, to be competitive in global markets, Singapore introduced wide-ranging measures from the outset to enhance the business environment. These measures included close attention to the maintenance of political and macroeconomic stability; measures to foster labour discipline and peaceful industrial relations; revamping the educational system (a legacy of British colonial rule) and labour training programmes to emphasise engineering, technical skills and industrial skills; development of industrial infrastructure; active investment promotion; and the provision of generous fiscal incentives. Liberal trade and FDI policies have also been a hallmark of Singapore's economic policy from independence, and there is no specific law on foreign investment.

One cannot, therefore, distinguish policy phases marked by legislative changes in FDI policy, or in the degree of openness of the economy, comparable to those in Malaysia and many other countries. What has evolved is the type of activity targeted for promotion, and the degree of sophistication of policy design and implementation.

Draconian measures were introduced in the 1960s to improve the political and industrial relations climate, with the detention of communists and the introduction of labour legislation to control the trade unions. These measures together with generous fiscal incentives and aggressive investment promotion led to a surge of manufacturing FDI inflows during 1968-73, capitalising on an initial period of US and European firms' relocation of some labour-intensive electronics assembly activities to low-wage "offshore" production sites in developing countries. Double-digit economic growth and the disappearance of unemployment ensued in Singapore.

FDI inflows declined sharply in 1974-76, however, as the collapse of the Bretton Woods system of fixed exchange rates, the first oil shock and global recession weakened the global investment climate, and the fall of South Vietnam to the communists weakened the political and investment climate in Southeast Asia. Stagflation and recession in the US and European economies in the late 1970s and early 1980s nevertheless fuelled a renewed surge of cost-cutting relocation of production, and FDI flows, to Singapore in 1978-84. Worsening labour shortages at home combined with emerging competition from lower-wage neighbours in labour-intensive industries, and growing problems of market access as protectionist pressures mounted in Singapore's principal OECD export markets, led the government in 1979 to launch a major restructuring programme to shift the economy into higher value-added, more capital-, skill- and technology-intensive activities. Investment promotion became more selective and targeted on the electronics industry, machinery and precision engineering, heavy engineering (but not automobiles), chemical process industries and R&D activities.

Sharp increases in firms' operating costs and a strengthening of the Singapore dollar led, however, to a loss of export competitiveness and a sharp drop in FDI inflows along with recession in 1985-86. Industrial restructuring was interrupted, and the government introduced major cost-cutting measures along with an aggressive new investment promotion drive.

FDI inflows recovered sharply from 1986, and economic restructuring resumed as considerable upgrading took place in both new and expansion investment projects. Key industries that developed in Singapore during the 1980s include speciality chemicals and pharmaceuticals, computer hardware and software, advanced electronic components, precision engineering and medical instruments. In the process, however, Singapore finds itself increasingly having to compete against OECD countries to attract high value-added and high-tech FDI.

47

In response, since the latter half of the 1980s, Singapore has increasingly targeted its investment promotion efforts on attracting FDI by smaller, but highly innovative, foreign firms. Seeking to capitalise on opportunities arising from the increasing globalisation of OECD-based corporate activity, and attuned as well to the potential importance of growing regional integration — the latter both as a stimulus to the development of Asian markets (at least until the recent crisis) and other major regional markets, and as a potential new source of competition, or possible hindrance, for access to markets in the other major regions — Singapore has repositioned its investment-attraction strategy to promote the country as "a total business centre with capabilities to support international companies in all aspects of their business"[67]. Simultaneously, Singapore seeks to promote a regional division of activities among ASEAN economies in which foreign and local investors are encouraged to locate, or relocate, labour-intensive production in neighbouring countries with more abundant labour and land, and to upgrade and automate production and locate their regional service centres and operations headquarters in Singapore. It sees its competitive advantage for attracting investors as lying in its skilled, flexible and English-speaking workforce, its highly efficient infrastructure and wide range of business and financial services, its cultural and business links with Asian Pacific countries, its administrative efficiency, and its political, social and macroeconomic stability. As Chia notes, however, such "a regional division of labour is not easy to achieve, as neighbouring countries also want the sophisticated segments of the value chain for themselves and seek actively to promote such investments. This is most evident in Malaysia's plan for the Multimedia Super Corridor"[68].

Implications

Generous fiscal incentives have been an integral part of Singapore's highly successful long-term FDI-attraction strategy since the 1960s, not least because it sees them as more flexible than many other policy instruments used to affect investment decisions. The Economic Development Board, established in 1961 to spearhead Singapore's economic development and more particularly its drive for industrialisation and the attraction of FDI, generally eschews financial subsidies except for training and R&D, while consistently making liberal use of fiscal incentives in the form of tax holidays and concessions. As Chia explains, "The Singapore government places great faith in the efficacy of tax incentives and uses them liberally in investment promotion to help shape the pace and direction of industrial development"[69]. Indeed, since the late 1970s, the EDB not only prioritises industries and activities in its investment promotion activities, it targets specific multinational companies for attraction to Singapore. As Chia thus observes, as well, "The EDB's list of priority industries ... indicates sectoral targeting and picking winners"[70].

Singapore's tax incentives have changed over the years in response to changing economic conditions. Tax holidays for "pioneer" manufacturing investments (i.e. in activities new to Singapore) were introduced in 1959, following their introduction in Malaya. Added since then have been tax incentives for industrial expansion, export promotion, industrial upgrading, and R&D. An investment tax credit scheme was introduced in 1979, again to promote upgrading, and the establishment of firms with long gestation periods. Additional tax incentives have also been introduced to promote investment in technologically more sophisticated industries and R&D activities.

These tax incentives are generally available to both foreign and local investors, and are applied both generally and on a discretionary, case-by-case basis. As in other countries, however, foreign investors tend in practice to be favoured by incentive schemes that are geared to large or technically advanced projects and to the promotion of exports.

There is little available evidence to suggest any escalation in recent years of FDI incentives in Singapore relative to the size of FDI inflows. Regrettably, we have found no data that would permit measurement of the values of those incentives, either overall or for major individual investment projects. Nor, apparently, have press reports advanced such figures in Singapore as they have in many other countries (perhaps reflecting less free or active local media, or perhaps due simply to the fact that Singapore has not attracted, nor sought to attract, the major automobile investment projects that have generally attracted such media attention elsewhere). One indicator, however unsatisfactory, may nevertheless be the ratio of the EDB's net annual operating expenditure to annual FDI inflows in manufacturing. That ratio remained relatively stable from 1985 to 1994 (the last year for which the ratio is available) at between 0.13 and 0.20 per cent.

Also noteworthy is the fact that, notwithstanding the numerous fiscal incentives Singapore offers to corporate investors, corporate income-tax revenue has risen over the years and the government has enjoyed a budget surplus, not only over current expenditures but also over its sizeable investment expenditures, for numerous years. That surplus, more than tax competition with other countries, has in turn made it possible for Singapore progressively to reduce the corporate income tax rate, from 40 per cent in the 1960s to 26 per cent today. This reduction in the corporate income tax rate must itself be seen as a major fiscal attraction to FDI. It also, of course, reduces the effectiveness of Singapore's many discretionary fiscal incentives.

Despite its long-standing and generous use of discretionary fiscal incentives to attract FDI, Singapore thus seems progressively to have been diminishing the relative importance it gives to such incentives in its overall policy approach to FDI. Like many countries, it seems to have been giving more attention to rules-based policies towards FDI — a subject we discuss in Chapter 4. This shift in policy emphasis has coincided with the growing competition for FDI which Singapore has faced in recent years from new and old members of ASEAN, from other developing and newly industrialised economies, and from OECD countries. What remains to be seen is whether the crisis that emerged in Asia in the latter half of 1997 will give new impetus to incentives-based competition for FDI in the region. If it does, Singapore appears well equipped to respond.

Competition in China[71]

China has moved quickly from its status as a country long closed to FDI, in 1979, to become, since 1993, the largest developing-country host to FDI — and, after the United States, the second largest host in the world. As of end-1997, China's estimated stock of FDI amounted to almost $220 billion. The ratio of that stock to China's GDP is high — almost 25 per cent — as FDI inflows have grown from an annual average of about $3 billion in 1986-91 to over $40 billion in 1996 and an estimated $45 billion in 1997[72]. Four-fifths of the FDI comes from other Asian economies, notably Hong Kong, and 90 per cent is located in China's coastal areas, the bulk of it in real estate and relatively labour-intensive manufacturing. FDI is now estimated to account for 17 per cent of China's industrial output, 12 per cent of its tax revenues, 41 per cent of exports, and 17 million jobs.

It was in 1979 that China turned to the "reform and open door" policy which emphasises the role of the external sector in national economic development. In addition to encouraging the expansion of trade, a central component of that policy has been to open the country to FDI on an incremental basis. In 1980, the central government established four Special Economic Zones, along the coast, which offered foreign investors significant tax holidays, low tax rates and relatively flexible administrative procedures. In 1983, the central government allowed provincial governments, autonomous regions and directly administered cities to approve FDI projects. In 1984, 14 coastal cities joined the Special Economic Zones as open areas, leading to a substantial FDI surge that year. In subsequent years, the authority to approve FDI projects up to $10 million per project has been extended to municipal and county-level governments.

Based on the relatively successful experience of the coastal areas in utilising FDI, in the early 1990s the central government began giving inland provinces the authority to pursue similar FDI-attraction policies. While coastal areas have continued to attract the bulk of FDI inflows, the overall effect of this incremental process of opening up to FDI has been increasingly to shift control over FDI authorisations from the central to local governments. Accompanying this shift has been a tendency towards FDI policy liberalisation, and a streamlining of approvals procedures, driven by sub-national governments' strong desire to attract FDI in order to speed up local development. The decentralisation process in FDI approvals has also generated competition among those governments to attract FDI.

During the 1980s and early 1990s, this competition mostly involved sub-national governments' competing within the central government's FDI policy framework, seeking to implement that policy more effectively and flexibly. Following the Communist Party's 1992 decision to develop China as a "socialist market" economy, rather than a centrally-planned economy, the central government has progressively lifted state control over investment planning, gradually reduced protection of state-owned enterprises, encouraged inter-firm competition, and committed itself to the development of a more transparent legal and regulatory system. This regulatory system

— virtually inexistent 15 years ago — comprises national laws on FDI and regulations to guide implementation of those laws, as well as a growing body of international investment-protection agreements.

The central government has taken a "proactive" approach to attracting FDI: it has only a negative list of industries where FDI is restricted or prohibited ("strategic" and information-technology-related industries) and it provides incentives for export-oriented and technologically advanced FDI projects. The definition of such industries is subject to the interpretation of local governments, to a considerable degree, so that those governments have some flexibility in their choice of projects for approval and for the granting of tax concessions — which creates opportunities both for competition among those governments, and for corruption. The export requirement (75 per cent in most Special Economic Zones) is also subject to local modifications, and, with the growing recognition of the need to attract FDI in services and in technologically more advanced industries, since 1996 the central government has begun progressively to implement a policy of "national treatment" whereby FDI-enterprises are allowed access to the domestic market in sectors where that access was previously denied or restricted. Today, already, it is estimated that most FDI-enterprises export less than 50 per cent of their production.

Fiscal incentives involve five types of taxes: profits tax, turnover tax, value-added tax, import duties and local tax. Turnover and value-added taxes are determined by the central government, but the local tax (3 per cent) is levied at the discretion of local governments, and is often reduced or eliminated as a means to compete with other local governments for FDI. The standard tax on corporate profits is 30 per cent, but is reduced to 15 per cent for Special Economic Zones and some economic development areas. Tax holidays are also granted, usually consisting of a 100 per cent exemption for the first two profit-making years and a 50 per cent exemption for the third year. Duty exemptions are also granted to imports in the case of export-oriented industries. Tax rebates for exports vary — and have been used as a policy alternative to varying the exchange rate for the purpose of encouraging exports.

Local governments can thus use fiscal incentives as a policy tool in competing with one another, but their ability to do so operates within important constraints set by the central government. Nor, reportedly, do local governments seek to depress local wages as a means to compete for FDI — although, it must be emphasised, China as a whole remains subject to strong international criticism for the restrictions it imposes on the right of workers to form trade unions and on the use of union funds for political purposes[73].

Rather, it appears, the most important cost determinant of FDI in China on which sub-national governments compete is *land*. Local governments are generally given the authority to make land grants (a lease period of up to 50 or 70 years) and to determine land-use fees. In joint ventures between local and foreign investors, the local partner's contribution to equity is often land. The cost of land and the conditions of land grants have thus become a pivotal tool in policy competition for FDI among local governments. (Interestingly, there is co-operation as well as competition among local governments in determining land-use fees, as they share information on those fees and average figures are published for particular regions every quarter.) Concessional rates on utilities charges are also used by local governments to compete for FDI.

Many local governments focus as well on the need to improve their physical infrastructure to attract FDI. A growing number also seek to attract FDI in infrastructure, including via "BOT" (Build, Operate, Transfer) agreements with foreign companies. The most widely used approach to competition continues, however, to be that of seeking to ensure potential investors of the administrative and operational efficiency of the approval process, including the provision of "one-stop" or "one-street" procedures and performance pledges. The results of these pledges still vary considerably, however, because they depend heavily on the effectiveness of co-operation and co-ordination among various departments and units within each government.

A particularly important recent development is the move by the central government, since April of 1996, to experiment with the "national treatment" of FDI-enterprises, which means allowing them access to the domestic market. Previously, incentives-based policies were the predominant means of competition for FDI among sub-national governments, notwithstanding their growing attention to the need for investment in infrastructure and human capital, and for rules and regulations to protect intellectual property rights as they became aware of the need to attract FDI in services and technologically advanced industries. However, the move towards "national treatment" of FDI-enterprises in terms of market access means that many of the tax concessions given to FDI-enterprises will progressively have to be withdrawn — thereby also limiting the possibility for sub-national governments to offer such concessions.

The period of "transition" or experimentation with national treatment is expected to last three to five years, and during this period those regions where national treatment does not apply can continue to offer tax concessions. In the regions where national treatment is applied, the power to attract FDI is expected to grow despite the withdrawal of tax concessions. Differences among regions in terms of what they can do to compete for FDI are thus likely to grow during the period of transition. Overall, however, the central government has begun to reverse the trend towards decentralisation of FDI policy, limiting the growth of local governments' flexibility to develop their own FDI policy instruments, while at the same time lifting important entry barriers to the domestic market.

A good illustration of how sub-national governments compete in China to attract FDI, and of how that competition has evolved over the 1980s and 1990s, is the experience of Shenzhen Special Economic Zone, in Guandong Province (a province that contains three of China's five Special Economic Zones and hosts about a third of all FDI in China, much of it from Hong Kong). The government of Shenzhen has long provided fiscal incentives to FDI-enterprises: a corporate income tax of 15 per cent on those enterprises, and their exemption from the 3 per cent local tax. It provides preferred FDI projects with concessional rents on factory premises, low land-use fees and long tenure (up to 70 years). In recent years, as rising wage and land costs have increased production costs in Shenzhen, the local authorities have moved to strengthen and upgrade the Zone's Foreign Investment Service Centre, which now provides a full range of services to FDI projects. They have also moved selectively to open the Zone to FDI in financial services, tourism and other services, and have abolished the export requirement for technologically advanced FDI projects.

Interviews of government officials and foreign investors undertaken for this study revealed that while Shenzhen officials consider incentives important to attract FDI, especially from Hong Kong, investors tended to point up the quality of Shenzhen's physical infrastructure, less bureaucratic administrative system, general business environment, and access to the domestic market as more important[74].

The Xiamen Special Economic Zone, in Fujian Province, provides another important example. Over the last two decades, its authorities have adopted a pioneering approach to attracting FDI — notably from Chinese Taipei. The government recognises the importance of policy competition with other locations in China, and offers incentives comparable to those available in Shenzhen. These include fiscal incentives, low rents for factory premises, low land-use fees and up to 50 years' tenure rights. A Foreign Investment Working Committee provides a wide range of services for FDI projects, and encourages FDI in infrastructure and high-tech industries. Since 1996, the government has moved progressively towards a policy of "national treatment", as in Shenzhen, by selectively allowing FDI in financial services and retailing.

The Xiamen government has paid particular attention to the development of local human resources — and has a well-developed education sector — as well as to environmental management and infrastructure development. In 1992, Xiamen ranked as one of the best cities in China in terms of overall development indicators and investment climate, and the local government prefers to adopt a long-term strategy on attracting FDI, emphasising the development of infrastructure and human resources and the creation of a favourable business climate. The foreign investors interviewed for this study seemed to be most impressed with these factors and with the experiment on granting national treatment — with a growing number of such major investors as Intel, Shell and Toshiba recently having expressed their intention to invest in Xiamen.

A third example is the experience of Dalian City, in Liaoning Province in north-eastern China, which was opened to FDI in 1985 as a "coastal economic development zone". Since the late 1980s, the provincial government has launched provincial regulations governing FDI on investment promotion (1987), land management (1989) and labour relations (1991) which are comparable to those in Guandong and Fujian provinces. Nevertheless, prior to 1992, Dalian city received less FDI inflows than expected, despite the incentives and other favourable FDI policies offered by the local government. Given the importance of FDI from Hong Kong and Chinese Taipei in total FDI flows to China at that time, local officials believe the main explanation was those investors' preference for Guangdong and Fujian because of their greater geographical proximity and cultural affinity.

More recently, the progressive move by the central government to open the domestic market is seen by Dalian officials as giving them a good opportunity to attract FDI in view of the huge market in north China. Japan and Korea, with their historical economic and geographical links to northeastern China, have become important sources of FDI. In 1995, Dalian ranked third among coastal cities as a host to FDI, after Shenzhen and Guanzhou.

Incentives continue to be the principal policy instrument to attract FDI in Dalian. The incentives, combined with relatively low labour and land costs in the area, have proved to be relatively effective according to local officials. The officials interviewed also noted the existence of complaints from local enterprises, who argue that the incentives given to foreign investors place them in a position of competitive disadvantage.

Dalian has also created an economic and technological development zone, a bonded zone, and a high-tech industrial village. As the only bonded zone in north China, the Dalian Bonded Zone is expected to attract foreign investors by providing a range of investment incentives and a good investment environment. While the foreign investors interviewed are quite optimistic about the future of investing in Dalian, especially in light of the market potential in north China, they expressed caution about expanding current FDI projects. Two important constraints appear to be the level of skills of available labour, and the weakness of existing distribution channels for serving the market in north China.

Data from these three examples — the Shenzhen and Xiamen Special Economic Zones and Dalian City — suggest that tax holidays account for about half the total amount of incentives given to foreign investors, with land concessions accounting for another 30 per cent, infrastructure 10 per cent, and "others" 10 per cent. The value of incentives offered per job-to-be-created was not found to be large by international comparison: figures on the order of $1 000 per job were obtained for recent FDI projects in the electronics and food industries.

In sum, while incentives-based competition is widespread among sub-national governments in China, it does not appear to have produced uncontrolled bidding wars to any significant degree. More worrisome is the extent to which the decentralisation of control over FDI approvals has been accompanied by the growth of regional disparities, on the one hand, and of rent-seeking and even corrupt practices by local officials, on the other. The good news, looking to the future, is that the central government's decision to move towards national treatment of FDI-enterprises, and to give foreign investors access to the domestic market, indicates a growing emphasis in China on rules-based forms of competition to attract FDI, notably including a strengthening of the legal system, reduced discrimination between foreign and domestic investors, and a reduced role for incentives-based competition.

Competition in India[75]

India hosts relatively little FDI. As recently as 1990, the stock of FDI in India amounted to less than $2 billion, with a ratio of FDI stock to GDP of barely 0.5 per cent[76]. Only in 1991 did India turn to a more liberal economic policy regime — and since then FDI inflows have begun to grow. From an average annual FDI inflow of less than $200 million in 1986-91, the inflow has risen to $2.4 billion in 1996 and an estimated $3.3 billion in 1997. Today, the ratio of FDI stock to GDP stands at about 2.6 per cent[77].

It is also since 1991 that inter-state competition to attract FDI has begun to heat up in India. As a World Bank publication recently noted, "The programme of stabilisation and reform underway since 1991 has radically changed the framework within which states' development policies are implemented. States can now attract private capital in such sectors as power, irrigation, ports, roads, and all areas of manufacturing, and it is their ability to attract private capital that now determines the states' growth performance. Development spending now ... complements rather than substitutes for the private sector. This is a radical departure from the pre-1991 period, when the volume of public development spending was the key determinant of a state's growth performance"[78].

To varying degrees, India's 25 state governments have moved since 1991 to woo private investors, especially foreign investors, with a broad range of incentives. The incentives include provisions for various sales-tax exemptions and tax-deferment schemes, capital grants and other direct financial support, including for project-specific infrastructure. They include reduced tariff rates for electric power and other utilities, and reductions of, or exemptions from, property taxes. Many state and local governments have also undertaken investment feasibility studies, and provide investors help in formulating project analysis.

The authors of the report on India undertaken for this study gathered extensive data on the incentive provisions announced by 16 states in 60 industrial categories[79]. These data were used to construct a composite incentives index for each state for two periods: the early 1990s, and the post-1993 period. They show considerable convergence or clustering among states in terms of the level of their incentives index[80]. They also show some increase in that level between the two periods[81]. Both patterns point to some intensification of incentives-based competition among states in India since 1991.

Interviews of corporate managers, also carried out by the authors of the report undertaken for this study, showed that investors' ranking of states by degree of "investor friendliness" did not correlate with the ranking of states by the level of their incentives index. The authors did however find a weak positive correlation between the ranking of states by level of their incentives index and states' ranking by the size of FDI inflows relative to the size of their economy[82]. This correlation suggests either that richer states tend to offer more incentives, and/or that incentives can have an impact when states' economic and political fundamentals are similar.

What the interviews showed most clearly was that the leading determinant of investors' decisions is the availability of good quality infrastructure — in transportation, energy, telecommunications and water[83]. Backing their findings with a regression of state-level incentives and infrastructure indices for 1993 against variation over 1994-96 in the level of investment relative to the size of a state's economy[84], the authors conclude that a state's provision of incentives can "play a significant role in attracting private investment if, and only if, the state has a certain level of infrastructure available to support [investors'] activities"[85].

The Ford-Mahindra Auto Plant

An in-depth case study of a recent investment project gives a useful perspective to these results. The project is a \$400 million investment to produce automobiles, largely for the Indian market, undertaken by Ford as a joint venture with the Indian firm, Mahindra, in which Ford holds a 90 per cent equity share and Mahindra a 10 per cent share. The investment is in a plant due to commence production in 1999, with an initial annual production capacity of 50 000 vehicles and expected to create 900 jobs.

According to the managers of Ford interviewed for this study, Ford did not consider any locations outside India for this project, but did consider several within the country. While Bangalore and the Delhi area were among the locations considered, the competition was mainly between sites in the states of Maharashtra and Tamil Nadu.

Ford managers noted that the state government of Maharashtra assumed that Ford would locate in Maharashtra, not least because it is the home state of the Mahindra group; they argued that the Maharashtra government seriously erred in that assumption. They explained that the site finally chosen, in Tamil Nadu, "is near an international airport, near an international seaport...and in our view Tamil Nadu has a more literate, more educated, work force and, perhaps more importantly, has a better labour-relations record than Maharashtra"[86]. Ford managers added that while "Maharashtra thought they were kings [and] we should just fall at their feet...Enron [a US energy company that was having trouble with the Maharashtra government] was at the back of our minds"[87].

Ford managers listed the most important factors in their location decision as follows. Of greatest importance were the availability of skilled labour and of a parts supplier base (both factors were ranked 9 by Ford managers on an importance-scale of ten), followed by the availability of infrastructure (ranked 8) and, in particular, proximity to a seaport and container terminal (the company expects to have significant exports and imports, and freight tends to be shipped by truck and ship rather than by air). The incentives provided by the Tamil Nadu government were next in importance (ranked 7). These include a 14-year exemption both from the state sales tax levied on vehicles sold within the state (equivalent to 11 per cent of the ex-factory price of vehicles) and from the sales tax levied by the central government on vehicles produced in but sold outside the state (equivalent to 4 per cent of the ex-factory price of vehicles, an amount to be paid by the state government on behalf of Ford-Mahindra) — with about 90 per cent of output expected to be sold outside the state. Additional incentives include provision by the state government of free-hold land, low-cost electric power (i.e. power tariff concessions) during four years, a water-supply scheme, and an offer to build a sewage plant. Ford also requested labour-training grants, which were refused, and provision by the state of a railway loading yard, which was still under discussion in 1998.

Less important factors cited by Ford managers included the proximity of an international airport and proximity to the target market (both ranked 3). While the lesser importance of proximity to an airport is due to the much greater importance of proximity to the seaport, as noted earlier, the lesser importance of proximity to the target market reflects the fact that India as a whole is the target market.

Among the incentives, financially the most important, by far, are the tax-relief incentives. Assuming vehicle sales of 50 000 units per year over the 14-year period of tax relief (a conservative estimate because capacity may be expanded during this period to 100 000 units), the value of "recurring" incentives, estimated at about $27 million per year, amounts to some $378 million. This amount is equivalent to $420 000 for each of the 900 jobs to be created (as shown in the Table at the end of this chapter); if, as the authors of the report do, one assumes a 12 per cent annual social discount rate, the value of these incentives still amounts to over $200 000 for each job likely to be created[88].

Also noteworthy is Ford's response to the concern expressed by the state's Pollution Control Board that the state government might not build a suitable sewage treatment facility, despite the state government's agreement with Ford to do so. The Pollution Control Board was therefore reluctant to issue a "No Objection Certificate" for construction of the plant. Ford decided to invest in the construction of the sewage facility on its own in order to expedite the issuance of the Certificate, and was thus able to obtain it.

Ford managers also explained that the nature of the title they were given to the land was an important factor in their location decision. The government of Tamil Nadu was not only able to make land available in a good location at a good price, it agreed to provide "free-hold" ownership as opposed to a lease. In contrast, the government of Maharashtra's unwillingness to provide such ownership was cited by Ford officials as a major reason for rejecting that state's offer.

Another reason cited was the labour problems Mahindra had been having at its factory in Maharashtra. Ford was thus desirous to select a location far from Mahindra's labour union.

The authors of the report also note that parts suppliers in Tamil Nadu appear to have played "a significant and proactive role" in presenting the case for their state's site as a desirable location, and that senior managers of these firms actively lobbied their state's government on behalf of Ford via their industry association. Ford is in turn making extensive efforts to have its suppliers locate near its plant in order to minimise the adverse effects of poor transportation and road networks. The authors further note that the combined efforts of the state government and the industry association "are likely to pay high dividends. Besides Ford, two other major auto companies — Hyundai and Mitsubishi — have also decided to locate [there]. Not only are these firms planning to source components from existing supplier firms, [they are] encouraging other auto component firms (foreign as well as Indian) to locate in the area. This is likely to result in a significant flow of fresh investment into the area"[89].

Despite the high financial cost to the state of the fiscal incentives provided, it is thus difficult to argue that the state would have been better off not to offer those incentives. Unfortunately, the authors of the report were unable to determine whether Ford was likely, or unlikely, to have undertaken the investment in Tamil Nadu in the absence of the state's offer to provide the relief from the central government's sales tax on cars sold outside the state. That fiscal incentive, alone, accounts for considerably more than half of the total estimated cost to the state of the incentives provided to attract the investment project. Had the investment been obtained without the state's providing that incentive, the authors estimate the social benefit/cost ratio of the project for the state would have been about 2; with the inclusion of that incentive, they estimate the benefit-cost ratio for the state to be about 0.8. Likewise, they calculate a net present social value of the project, including incentives, in the range of minus $30 million to minus $50 million; absent state relief from the central government's sales tax on vehicles sold outside the state, they estimate the project's net present social value would have been in the range of (plus) $50 million to $100 million[90].

Finally, as regards the question of how inter-state competition to attract FDI affects the environment, and referring to Ford's decision to invest in its own sewage treatment facility, the authors conclude that such competition "does not necessarily create downward pressure on environmental standards, at least in the Indian case"[91].

What the authors do not mention, but their findings clearly suggest, is that in India, as in many other countries, competition among sub-national governments to attract FDI tends to exacerbate rather than to ameliorate long-term growth differentials and income inequalities among regions within the country.

Incentives-based Competition in OECD Countries: An Overview

The flow of FDI to OECD countries — most of it coming from other OECD countries — rose from an annual average of $117 billion (81 per cent of global inflows) in 1985-90, to $228 billion (57 per cent of global inflows) in 1997. While the share of global FDI flows going to OECD countries has thus diminished, largely in favour of developing and emerging economies in Asia and Latin America, that share remains large, and the volume of FDI going to OECD countries has risen significantly.

Many governments in OECD countries, notably at the sub-national level, compete actively with incentives to attract FDI. This is the case both in North America and in Europe, where the diversity of experience with incentives-based competition is considerable. No study of incentives-based competition would therefore be complete without a careful look at that competition in OECD countries, both because it affects global competition for FDI — potentially affecting competition in non-OECD countries, and between those countries and OECD countries — and because it offers important lessons of experience for developing and emerging economies.

This section provides an overview of incentives-based competition in the United States, Western Europe and Canada. FDI inflows to the United States rose from an annual average of $49 billion (35 per cent of global inflows) in 1985-90, to $91 billion (23 per cent of global inflows) in 1997. Corresponding figures for Western Europe — including intra-European FDI — were $56 billion (40 per cent of global inflows) in 1985-90, and $114 billion (29 per cent) in 1997. Canada received $5 billion per year on average (4 per cent of global inflows) in 1985-90, and $8 billion (2 per cent of global inflows) in 1997.

Japan, in contrast, has received only a fraction of 1 per cent of global FDI inflows: less than $0.4 billion per year on average in 1985-90, and about $3 billion in 1997[92].

The overall pattern of competition for FDI is one of active incentives-based competition in the United States by sub-national — especially state — governments, in Europe by both national and sub-national governments, and in Canada by provincial governments.

Competition in the United States[93]

The very large size of the US economy and the traditional ease of capital movements both into and out of the country go far to explain the huge size of FDI in the United States (with a stock of over $720 billion FDI, the country hosts more FDI stock than the next three largest hosts — the United Kingdom, China and France — combined). But it is noteworthy, for our purposes, that for many years the United States was a much larger source of outward investment than it was a recipient of inward investment; in the 20th century, only since the mid-1980s has inward FDI grown rapidly. (Inflows actually surpassed outflows in the 1980s, though not in the 1990s, when outflows have also been large[94].) FDI accounts today for over 5 million jobs in the United States, for over $140 billion in US exports, and for some 7.7 per cent of GDP.

Why the sudden surge of growth of FDI into the United States over the last 15 years? Much of the answer must be found, again, in the size and openness of the US economy, at a time when globalisation has been surging. This time, unlike the previous wave of globalisation during the 1950s and 1960s (when US firms were practically the only ones able to multinationalise their investments), significant numbers of firms based in other countries — notably in Europe and Asia — have been able to invest in the United States[95]. Their motivation to do so is also due, of course, to particular US strengths in technology and capital markets (both influenced by government policies) and to the generally business-friendly US policy environment, with its ease of corporate chartering, generally limited and predictable regulations, and modest tax burdens.

However, these business-friendly policies, it must be stressed, are not part of a national scheme to attract FDI. They reflect the long-standing pro-business culture of the United States, and the political effectiveness of local entrepreneurs, investors and managers who have sought rules and regulations to promote and accommodate domestic investment.

One could thus argue, as Donahue observes, that the US government's success at rules-based competition to attract FDI, although "accidental" or "inadvertent", is nevertheless so complete that the government has no need to engage in incentives-based competition. Such competition does, indeed, remain "all but unheard-of" at the federal level[96]. But, as Donahue also observes, there are forces flowing from the United States' federal structure that work to augment the country's attraction to FDI. First, while the federal government also rarely engages consciously in rules-based competition, many of the rules that matter most to investors are set not by the federal government but by the states, and to a lesser degree by cities and community governments. These rules frequently are designed to attract investment. Second, the incentives-based competition that is so unheard-of at the national level is a mainstay of state governments' activity. Our focus will therefore be on incentives-based competition for corporate investment as a whole (domestic and foreign) pursued in the United States by state governments.

Trends

No public agency collects data on the fiscal and financial incentives given to investors in the United States, and, as elsewhere, both governments and recipients tend to obscure the details and sometimes the very existence of incentive packages. Specifics are often "left to negotiation", and negotiations are often "done in a clandestine manner"[97]. Survey data collected at the level of individual states nevertheless provide strong evidence of an intensification of inter-state competition to attract investment since the late 1970s. Somewhat at odds with the UNCTAD report's affirmation that financial incentives are used more than fiscal incentives in OECD countries (although, it must be emphasised, the UNCTAD report refers mainly to the actions of national governments) these data also suggest that state governments in the United States devote three to twelve times as much money to fiscal incentives as they spend on more direct economic development programmes and financial incentives[98].

Thus, for example, data on the number of states offering various types of incentives show those numbers doubling, roughly, between 1977 and 1996[99]. The average number of incentive programmes in each state has also more than doubled[100]. A survey of over 200 major US corporate executives reports that in 1995, almost 80 per cent of their firms were receiving location incentives — the most common being property-tax rebates (51 per cent), income-tax credits (48 per cent) and sales-tax exemptions or rebates (35 per cent) — and 73 per cent saw incentives to be more freely available than five years earlier[101].

Also indicative of an intensification of inter-state competition to attract major corporate investment projects — projects which have predominantly been foreign-owned — is the steady and substantial rise in the approximate cost of incentives per job directly created in the ten major new automobile plants established in the United States between the late 1970s and the mid-1990s. Estimates show that cost to have risen, more or less in a straight line, from roughly $4 000 per job in the late 1970s and early 1980s to some $168 000 per job paid by Alabama in the early 1990s to attract the Mercedes plant[102] (these estimates are also shown in the Table at the end of this chapter).

While state governments are competing to attract corporate investment as a whole, and not specifically *foreign* corporate investment, there nevertheless has been a close parallel between the intensification of inter-state competition and the accelerated growth of inward FDI in the United States. The latter growth is visible, for example, in the rise in the share of total private employment accounted for in the United States by foreign-owned firms — a share that has risen from 1.8 per cent in 1977 to over 5 per cent in the early 1990s and 4.8 per cent today. Foreign-owned firms' share of new job *creation* has thus been quite high, and that fact in turn goes far to explain the "paradox" that while states compete to attract domestic investors as much or more than to attract foreign investors[103], the latter have been highly "over-represented" (relative to their contribution to the total stock of investment and jobs in the United States) in the high-profile state bidding-contests to attract major investment projects in recent years.

Whereas most US firms are already "rooted" somewhere in the United States (and branch-plant expansions are relatively rare and relocations even more so), new entrants into the United States are likely to be open to at least a few alternative investment sites — it is also generally in their interest at least to *appear* to be open, if only to attract more incentives — and are thus more likely to be perceived by competing governments as "in play". Indeed, while there is little evidence that the intensification of inter-state competition has helped in any significant way to increase the flow of FDI into the United States, there may well be a causal effect working in the opposite direction, i.e. the accelerated growth of FDI inflows from the mid-1980s may well have helped to stimulate the intensification of competition to attract investment as states sought to make sure they would get "their share" of the jobs likely to be associated with the major new investment projects.

Also noteworthy is how similar the incentive packages appear to have been, both among states and — except for the rising cost — over time. The typical package, certainly in the auto industry, includes exemptions from various state and local taxes along with subsidised site purchase or preparation (often including dedicated infrastructure such as road and rail links, water supply and treatment, etc.) and significant funding for workers' training.

There is thus little empirical support for the theory (discussed in more detail in our chapter on rules-based competition) which holds that in competing to attract investors, states are serving as "laboratories" to test alternative approaches to the "allocation" of investment sites through a process of *tâtonnement* or "experimentation" that leads to the survival and spread of the most efficient approaches[104]. Rather, as one study notes, with states offering "essentially similar incentive packages in terms of the types of benefits being provided, their next recourse is to offer more of each"[105]. The best metaphor is thus neither the "laboratory" nor the "dating game", as Donahue puts it, but the interaction of supply and demand. Referring to the auto industry, he notes, "So long as state officials perceive auto assembly plants as desirable, and so long as many states can offer acceptable sites ... there will be a seller's market for automaking jobs"[106] — and, one might add, a buyer's market for auto plant sites.

Nor is there much evidence that the price that states are paying to attract investment and jobs is serving the cause of creating jobs in the geographical areas that need them most. (This is important because one of the strongest arguments for the use of incentives is that they can be used to steer jobs to areas that most need them.) Many of the states that have used incentives successfully to attract major investment projects in recent years are, indeed, states that suffer from above-average levels of unemployment — making "job creation" all the more powerful as a political slogan in those states to justify paying the price of incentives — but the actual location of the investment project, in most cases, has been in a part of the state characterised by less unemployment, sometimes substantially less, than in the state as a whole.

It is equally hazardous, however, to infer — as one might be tempted to do from all that has been said so far — that the price states are paying via incentives to attract investors is too high. The reason it is hazardous is that just as secrecy makes it difficult to measure the cost of incentives, so are the benefits of incentives also very difficult to measure — both in theory and in practice.

Some critics of incentives argue, for example, that politicians often probably believe they are not putting public resources to their best use, but cynically count on fooling enough voters to score political points by attracting high-profile investments. Careful economic analysis shows, however, that even for the Mercedes investment in Alabama, the net present value of several years of wage benefits alone may exceed, and thus justify, the price of the incentives paid. Certainly a cheaper deal, if attainable, would have been better for Alabama. But it is quite possible that Alabama is better off with the deal it got than if Mercedes had gone to another state. As Donahue notes, "it is difficult to counsel politicians that their constituents' interests — let alone their own electoral interests — are well served by standing aloof from the fray [of bidding wars]"[107].

Effects and Implications

The prevailing view on the ability of incentives to affect firms' investment-location decisions has also evolved since the early 1980s, when the broad consensus among academics, which had built up over years, was that states were largely powerless to alter business location decisions (notwithstanding the frequency with which state politicians already acted otherwise)[108]. Following his thorough review of the literature, covering both a dozen surveys of what managers say about the effects of public policies on firms' location decisions and 17 econometric studies that attempt to discern not what firms say but what they actually do in response to different public policies, Donahue concludes that "recently the weight of opinion has shifted, and experts are generally more respectful of the view that states can attract or repel private-sector investment through taxing and spending decisions"[109]. The reasons for this shift range from the many factors that tend to render investment locales increasingly good substitutes for one another — such as improvements in transportation and communications, and the evolution in demand towards services and products with higher ratios of value to weight — to the impact of mergers and acquisitions on reducing the number of firms anchored to a particular locale by family or cultural ties, and "globalisation" and the growing number of foreign entrants that also have no such ties. Intensifying competition and pressure on profit margins also make investors more sensitive to taxes and hungrier for subsidies — and their perceptions that others are receiving incentives further strengthens their desire to do likewise lest they suffer a competitive disadvantage.

If state and local governments' policies and incentives do indeed have more influence on firms' investment-location decisions than they did in the past — and this enhanced influence may be a further reason why inter-state competition is heating up in the United States — what are the implications for public policy? What, if anything, should governments — state, local, federal — do in response, individually and/or collectively, to protect the public interest? Donahue points up four broad options.

One option might be for individual governments to "opt out" of competition. The mainstream view among economists, shared by more than a few politicians, is that states and communities should concentrate on general policies to address the fundamentals and not fiddle with special deals to attract capital. Unfortunately, while this view makes sense in theory, the distinction between "general policies" and "special deals" tends to break down in practice. Intensifying inter-state competition also alters the evolution of general policies, and it affects how those policies are interpreted and applied. (Changes in Massachusetts' tax code in the mid-1990s, for example, were triggered by threats from a major manufacturer and a major financial-services corporation to shift investments to more accommodating states; those changes have nevertheless been depicted as enlightened fiscal policy reform.) Nor is it clear, as noted in reference to the high price of the incentives Alabama paid to attract Mercedes, that individual states are not better off paying the high costs incentives can entail than they would be if they attempted unilaterally to "opt out" of competition. The prisoner's dilemma they face is made all the more effective by the significant potential opportunity costs — which are also difficult to measure — of *not* competing for a major investment project.

A second option might be to compete, but only with incentives which clearly generate important spillover benefits for the host economy, as opposed to mere transfers to investors. These might include public spending on training and research, subsidising investments in physical infrastructure with significant benefits likely to accrue to the broader community (even when packaged to suit particular investors), and offering incentives only to attract particularly desirable individual investors. (They may also include "clawback provisions" that require subsidised firms to reimburse subsidies if, for example, commitments on the number, quality or duration of jobs are not met.) Unfortunately, however, the key distinction — this time between incentives with and those without important spillover benefits — once again makes more sense in theory than in practice. While it is in the interest of governments to push incentives with likely spillovers, it is generally in the interest of potential investors to seek out incentives that respond more directly to their needs for goods and services that they would otherwise have to pay for themselves. As Donahue observes, "It is somewhat inconsistent to conclude that states are compelled by competitive pressure to accommodate business demands for incentives, yet are in a position to stipulate the form those incentives will take. ... Mobile investment capital in a position to insist on tax breaks or subsidies as a condition of creating or preserving jobs ... is often in a position to insist on the form in which assistance is delivered."[110]

Similar reasons probably explain why incentives do not appear to have been used with any effectiveness in the United States to steer investments (and associated jobs) to areas especially plagued by poverty or unemployment. As Donahue observes, "If firms are convinced that tax breaks and other incentives are ubiquitous, so that their rivals are already advantaged by location inducements — as were four out of five corporate officials responding to a 1995 Peat-Marwick survey — they might see their own benefits as merely levelling the playing field, and understandably refuse to take on extra costs (such as locating in disadvantaged areas) as a condition of receiving such assistance"[111]. The best available research suggests, indeed, that "incentives do not level the playing field [and that it is] difficult to argue that two decades of competition has produced a more efficient pattern of location inducements"[112].

A third option might be to forge inter-state alliances, and thus seek more collective strength for state governments *vis-à-vis* investors through unity. One should not, of course, lose sight of the fact that investors and people living in different states share many interests — in good education and training policies, reliable modern infrastructure, clean air and water, fair and efficient government, etc. — but it is equally true that there will always be some real or potential differences "at the margin", such as on priorities for public spending or on how the tax burden should be shared. How those differences are resolved depends heavily on bargaining leverage, and that leverage is very sensitive to the relative mobility of investors (greater mobility increases their bargaining leverage). Thus, just as workers can fortify their bargaining power *vis-à-vis* employers by forming unions and firms gain market power (if unchecked by competition authorities) by forming cartels, so can governments form alliances to bargain with investors over incentives.

Many attempts have in fact been made to forge such alliances in the United States. Examples include small groups of contiguous states both in the greater New York region and in the industrial Midwest, and the 1993 National Governors' Association's adoption of non-binding "guidelines for the de-escalation of inter-state bidding wars" which called for the exchange of information on incentive packages offered, and the use of incentives likely to have spillover benefits. But the prisoner's dilemma makes any such alliance fragile and unstable, a problem that is only exacerbated by the facts that the cast of characters changes as elected officials change, and that investment incentives come in so many different forms (some explicit, some covert, and some depicted as general economic policy reforms) which makes it relatively easy to defect unnoticed. Experience shows that "most alliances of this sort either collapse amid recriminations or are (by tacit consensus) rendered dead letters not long after their ratification"[113].

A fourth option, finally, might be to impose federal limits on competition. Indeed, the prisoner's dilemma nature of the problem suggests that federal limits might be the only serious option. There certainly is precedent, moreover, as the founding fathers of the United States, witnessing states in the 1780s squandering potential bargaining leverage with trading partners through separate dealings, arranged for federal control of trade in the US Constitution. Today, the time may thus have come to declare investment, like trade, a federal responsibility and pre-empt state governments' efforts to lure capital. As economists Graham and Krugman noted already in their 1989 study on FDI into the United States: "States would be well served if their power to grant investment incentives were simply abolished"[114].

The analogy to trade is nevertheless limited by the fact that state governments' incentives target domestic investors as much as they do foreign investors. Federal attempts to limit states' use of incentives to attract foreign investors without affecting their efforts to attract domestic investors would almost certainly tend to be ineffective, unacceptably intrusive, or both, because they would require a precise and circumscribed assertion of federal authority that is hardly compatible with the vast range of policies that can be used to attract investment. The Supreme Court, moreover, has proven reluctant to limit business rivalry among states — although some legal scholars also see investment incentives as more vulnerable to legal challenge than the record might suggest[115].

An alternative approach might be federal legislation that does not seek to pre-empt but to dampen competition among the states by, for example, taxing investors' income from incentives — conceivably at a high rate — in order to blunt or nullify the effectiveness of incentives. Here again, however, the difficulty to distinguish in practice between "incentives" and "general policies" means, as Donahue explains, that "federal action to deter specific incentives would require some procedure to determine precisely *which* policies should be counted as targeted incentives subject to federal sanctions on states or firms, and which should be construed as benignly general policies. This process would presumably involve some combination of federal bureaucrats, lawyers, and judges attempting to make fine distinctions on complex issues where billions of dollars depend on the decision. [Such processes] seldom present very efficient or edifying spectacles"[116].

Any legislative approaches to federal action would also have to prove themselves politically acceptable. Both companies and states tend to oppose federal action to curb inter-state competition. When the federal government's General Accounting Office surveyed state officials in 1980 on their views on restrictions on location incentives, even assuming the restrictions applied only to bidding for foreign investors, two-thirds of the 47 states responding (i.e. 31 states) were "strongly opposed" and another 17 per cent (8 states) were "opposed"; of the remaining 9 states 8 were "neutral" and only one was "mildly in favour" of the idea.

What explains this political opposition to federal limits on inter-state competition by state officials? Donahue advances four possible explanations. One is that state officials may fear excessive federal intrusion and conclude that "the cure of co-ordination would be worse than the disease of competition". Another is that while officials may see the impact of incentives competition as negative for the country as a whole, they believe their own state gains from it. A third is that they see short-term gains in terms of the political rewards they reap from "creating jobs" while the costs are spread over time and partly borne by their successors in office. (What these three explanations have in common, of course, is the view that state and local politicians and government officials desire to retain and perhaps expand their power.) A fourth explanation, on the other hand, might be that more than a few state officials actually believe inter-state competition for investment to be good for the country, either because they subscribe to the "laboratory" theory mentioned above, or to the "positive-sum game" line of reasoning cited in Chapter 1.

Donahue himself clearly remains sceptical about the benefits of incentives-based competition for investment in the United States, as do most other authors[117]. We return to the issue of rules-based competition for investment in Chapter 3.

Competition in Western Europe[118]

If the United States hosts more FDI today than any other country, with 20 per cent of the global stock, Western Europe is the main regional host of FDI, with almost 40 per cent of the global stock (including intra-European FDI). That share rose from 33 per cent in 1985 to a peak of 44 per cent in 1990, due notably to the "announcement effect" of the European Community's Single Market programme, before settling at its current level. Central and Eastern Europe, on the other hand, still host relatively little FDI (about 1.8 per cent of the global stock) although the amount has grown from about $2.5 billion in 1989, when the Berlin Wall fell, to over $62 billion today.

The United Kingdom alone hosts over a fifth of all FDI stock in Europe ($274 billion out of almost $1.3 trillion at end-1997) followed by France ($174 billion), Belgium-Luxembourg ($143 billion), Germany ($138 billion), the Netherlands ($128 billion), Spain ($111 billion), Italy ($79 billion) and Sweden ($44 billion). The ratio of inward FDI stock to GDP ranges from highs of about 46 per cent in Belgium-Luxembourg, 30 per cent in the Netherlands and 21 per cent in both Ireland and the United Kingdom, to lows of below 6 per cent in Germany, barely over 6 per cent in Portugal and about 7 per cent in Italy and Finland. The ratios are about 18 per cent in Switzerland and Spain, 14 per cent in Sweden and 10 per cent in France — and about 13 per cent for Western Europe as a whole (as compared to 8 per cent in the United States, 22 per cent in Canada, and less than 1 per cent in Japan). The ratio is 6 per cent in Central and Eastern Europe as a whole, though it ranges from 33 per cent in Hungary, around 14 per cent in the Czech Republic and 10 per cent in Poland, to barely over 1 per cent in Russia[119].

While European governments' attitudes towards inward FDI have clearly become more "FDI-friendly" on the whole since the 1970s — a change most noteworthy as regards FDI from outside Europe — one can broadly distinguish three groups of countries today in terms of their demonstrated eagerness to attract FDI. One group has consistently sought to attract FDI and to maximise its benefits for the host country. This group includes the United Kingdom and Ireland, the Benelux countries and Spain. Another group comprises countries that until recently were relatively unwelcoming or even hostile towards FDI but now actively pursue policies to attract it; this group includes France, the Scandinavian countries, Portugal, Greece and the ex-socialist Central European countries (within Europe, at least, it is perhaps the marked policy shift by these countries that most feeds perceptions today of growing policy competition to attract FDI). A third group of countries, including Germany, Italy and Switzerland, continues to be relatively uneager to attract FDI.

In Europe, as in the United States, sub-national governments, such as those of Scotland and Wales in the United Kingdom, are among the most active competitors, and providers of incentives, to attract FDI. In contrast to the United States, however, national governments also widely compete to attract investment; and at the same time — also in marked contrast to the United States — limits have been imposed on incentives-based competition ever since the European Economic Community was created, in 1957, with the signing of the Treaty of Rome. That Treaty gives the European Commission significant powers to limit the ability of member states of the Community (now the Union[120]) to offer subsidies to firms and investors.

The legal bases for EU policy to control the supply of subsidies — referred to in the jargon of the Treaty as "State aids" — are two articles in the Treaty which provide for a general ban on fiscal and financial subsidies to industry as a whole, on the one hand, and give the Commission wide-ranging discretionary powers to grant exceptions to that ban, on the other. There are no rules that relate to the use of subsidies specifically to attract investment, or that relate to the nationality of potential recipients — i.e. neither subsidies to foreign investors nor subsidies to investment as a whole are specifically targeted — but the rules clearly reflect a recognition by the authors of the Treaty that uncontrolled subsidies could undermine the objective of achieving a Common Market[121].

There are three basic types of EU rules on government subsidies: rules that limit subsidies for specific sectors which governments have perceived as "strategic" and thus sought to develop locally (e.g. synthetic fibres, automobiles) but which suffer from overcapacity; so-called "horizontal rules" on subsidies for small and medium-size enterprises (SME) and for certain types of activity, such as R&D and protection of the environment, which have important "public good" characteristics of a cross-sectoral nature; and rules on member states' assistance for poorer regions. The only general exceptions the Commission allows with respect to the overall ban are for subsidies ("State aids") to favour smaller firms (SME), on the one hand, and to favour poorer regions, on the other.

The result has been virtually to exclude the possibility for EU governments to provide investment incentives to large investment projects, whether domestic or foreign-owned, *except* for projects located in regions or areas designated by the Commission as "least-favoured" regions and/or "development" areas. Least-favoured regions are regions where per capita GDP is no more than 75 per cent of EU-wide per capita GDP (which currently account for some 22.7 per cent of the EU population); development areas, which tend to be smaller units than "regions", are poorer or less developed areas relative to the national average within each member state (and account for about 24 per cent of the EU population)[122].

The Commission's policy is that governments can provide incentives ("State aids") worth no more than 50 per cent (recently reduced from 75 per cent) of the value of an investment project's "eligible" costs — costs which basically correspond to the value of fixed assets — in least-favoured regions, and usually no more than 20 per cent (recently reduced from 30 per cent) of such costs in development areas. member states must notify the Commission in advance of any programme to offer incentives, and it is for the Commission, not member states, to decide whether a programme qualifies for exception from the general ban on investment subsidies. Commission approval of such a programme normally constitutes a "block" exception from the need to notify the Commission of incentives awarded under the programme — other than in some very "sensitive" sectors (e.g. steel, cars, synthetic fibres) and for very large investment projects; and the majority of incentives are provided in conjunction with such programmes.

National programmes nominally designed to favour the development of poorer regions and areas, and those suffering from high unemployment, have thus been the key vehicle for incentives-based competition for large investment projects among national and sub-national EU governments. Moreover, much as in the United States, it is often to attract *foreign* investors that governments compete most actively — not because of the investors' nationality *per se* (sometimes, indeed, despite it) but because, compared to domestic investors, foreign investors are often perceived as more mobile and more likely, when entering the country, to create significant numbers of new jobs. FDI projects tend on average to be larger than domestic investment projects, as well as more mobile, which also gives them more bargaining power in negotiations that determine so-called "award rates", i.e. the value of incentives relative to the amount of the investment[123].

Development assistance to less-favoured regions and areas in the form of investment subsidies, particularly capital grants to investment projects, has thus become the main type of incentive used to attract FDI. Such grant assistance is offered by all EU governments except Denmark (which offers no formal alternative) and constitutes the core of most governments' regional development assistance programmes. Nearly 80 per cent of all "greenfield" FDI in Ireland receives such assistance, according to data for the late 1980s, and roughly half the value of all regional development aids in Great Britain goes to FDI, according to data covering the years from 1984 to 1995, for example[124].

Intensification of Competition?

While competition among governments in Europe to attract FDI is undoubtedly intense — and by all accounts governments see their main competitors as other countries and regions in Europe[125] — the question of whether that competition is *intensifying* finds no clear answer. Part of the reason it does not is, as always, the lack of data due to the confidential nature of incentive agreements between governments and investors, but what evidence does exist also fails to suggest a clear answer.

On the one hand are the signs of intensifying competition. These include a notable increase in recent years in the number of investment-promotion agencies, including the creation of new national agencies in Sweden, Denmark, Finland and Greece. Also, many existing national and regional agencies have expanded their network of offices, including overseas, and some agencies, as in France, have gained greater autonomy *vis-à-vis* other government departments along with a greater share of FDI policy resources. There is also suggestive evidence in the form of press reports that cite apparently high costs of incentive packages offered for individual investment projects. A case in point is the incentives package for Hyundai's 1996 semi-conductor investment in Scotland, whose cost was not released by the UK government but was reported to be about $190 000 per job directly to be created by the investment. Both Germany and Austria reportedly made even higher offers, but failed to make the investor's final shortlist of candidate sites because of higher production costs[126].

Other examples, as shown in the table at the end of this chapter, include the 1991 Ford-VW investment in a new automotive plant in Portugal, whose incentive package for the 5 000 jobs directly to be created reportedly cost more than $265 000 per job, and the 1997 investment by VW in Germany (Lower Saxony) to modernise two plants whose incentives package, to safeguard 2 300 jobs, reportedly cost about $180 000 per job[127].

It is logical, moreover, to expect an intensification of competition for FDI as the post-1985 policy build-up to the Single Market swept away many forms of investment protection within Europe at a time when unemployment levels were rising to unprecedented levels in many countries on the continent. Not only do governments see other regions and countries within Europe as their main competitors, they often target largely the same sectors — notably autos, electronics and pharmaceuticals — which means that competition for the available investment in those sectors is very intense. One visible result has been a growing similarity of governments' targeting strategies, along with growing experience and sophistication of promotion methods, including greater attention to retaining existing investors (notably in Germany), which effectively intensify competition. Another result has been to increase the promotional activity of local governments, whose role, though still limited compared to that of national and regional governments, has grown rapidly, especially in the provision of workers' training and subsidised property and site preparation for major investment projects — thereby intensifying competition as well.

The advent of European Monetary Union and the single currency can only add to the intensification of competition as well, as intra-EU currency-exchange risks disappear and the European economy becomes ever more integrated.

Indeed, following the introduction of the euro, taxation is expected to become a particularly hot issue as pressure builds on EU governments to harmonise their tax systems. But already there is evidence of intensifying incentives-based competition in the form of tax competition — although, it must be emphasised, this competition involves governments' seeking to attract relatively liquid and highly mobile forms of capital, such as savings and financial flows and portfolio investment, as much as (or more than) to attract direct investment. There is evidence, for example, of a shift in the incidence of taxation in EU countries, especially in the early 1990s, caused at least in part by intensifying tax competition, in which labour's share of the overall tax burden has risen from below 35 per cent in 1980 to over 40 per cent in 1994, while capital's share has fallen over the same period from roughly 45 to about 35 per cent[128]. Corporate income-tax rates have also tended to decline, and to converge to some extent, since the early 1980s[129].

On the other hand, however, there is also substantial evidence that fails to support the hypothesis of intensifying incentives-based competition to attract FDI. Particularly important are data i) on the average award rates of incentive packages; and ii) on government spending on incentives. Both sets of data are consistent with the claim of most investment-promotion agencies in Europe that while competition is intense, it has not led to bidding wars[130].

Of course, theoretically, award rates are limited by the Commission's ceilings on State aids, which set limits on the percentage of investment projects' eligible costs that can be covered by incentive packages. One thus might not expect to see an upward trend in award rates even in a context of intensifying competition. The problem, however (i.e. the reason the evidence on award rates is inconsistent with the hypothesis of intensifying competition), is, first, that actual award rates tend to remain far below the Commission's ceilings (i.e. those ceilings do not appear to act as constraints) and, second, that average award rates have actually tended to *fall* over the last 15 years.

Specifically, the highest legal ceiling applies to much or all of Ireland, Portugal, Spain, Greece and the south of Italy; lower ceilings apply to designated poorer regions and areas in more prosperous countries. The data on average *actual* award rates, on the other hand, show a decline in France from over 13 per cent in 1984-87 to below 6 per cent in 1992-95 — over a period when FDI was surging in France — and show comparable declines in most other EU countries. Only in Germany did the average actual award rate clearly rise — from below 9 per cent to over 16 per cent in those same years — and that rise was due to the inclusion of Germany's eastern *Länder* in the latter years (award rates in the western *Länder* have fallen steadily)[131].

Government expenditures on incentives have also declined in a majority of countries. Data on per capita spending in recipient regions and areas from 1980 to 1993 (the last year for which we have data[132]) show a decline in France from $20 to $7, in the Netherlands from $66 to $9, in Great Britain from $76 to $28, in Northern

Ireland from $198 to $48, and in Ireland from $131 to $50. They show a rise in Germany from $36 to $105, in Luxembourg from $75 to $105 and in Italy from $223 to $480 — but these figures also point up the huge disparity among countries, which does little in itself to support the hypothesis of intensifying competition.

Measured as a share of GDP, moreover, government expenditures on investment incentives range, according to data for the early 1990s, from a high of less than 0.6 per cent in Ireland, to below 0.05 per cent in France, the Netherlands, the United Kingdom, Denmark and the western *Länder* of Germany (with shares lying between 0.1 and 0.2 per cent in Belgium, Italy, Spain and Germany's eastern Länder[133]). By way of comparison, most EU governments spent more than 0.5 per cent of GDP during this same period on industrial R&D measures and projects. In no case can government spending levels on investment incentives be described as dangerously high relative to GDP.

Some authors see these downward trends in award rates and per capita government spending on investment incentives as "a tribute to the controls on regional incentive spending that operate at the Community level"[134]. Others argue that the real constraints on investment incentives have been the growing budget constraints faced by national governments — constraints also reflected in regional-aids programme-managers' growing insistence on "obtaining value for money spent" — caused notably by the increasing demands placed on social-security systems as unemployment has risen (higher nation-wide unemployment has sometimes also made it more difficult to defend special assistance to particular regions). Some argue that "the ceilings authorised by the Commission are largely theoretical and of limited impact in terms of disciplining regional aids"[135].

Finally, the impact of incentives on investors' locational decisions is unclear. Investor surveys in Europe, as in the United States, repeatedly find that financial incentives have limited significance in investors' location decisions. Yet, as Bachtler *et al.* report, "it is clear from individual accounts of competition for larger projects that substantial awards can have a major role in winning investments ... "[136]. More broadly, there is some evidence in France and the United Kingdom of a positive correlation between the value of incentives that investors of large projects have been offered to locate in specific regions and the number of large job-creating FDI projects that have located in those regions; but there is little such evidence in Spain, Italy or Germany[137].

It may well be true, furthermore, as Bachtler *et al.* argue, that, "[t]his uncertainty has not only allowed policy makers considerable scope for using incentives, [it] may have encouraged competition between governments in attracting FDI projects"[138]. And, they add, "it is by no means clear that regional incentive policies are able to achieve their primary objective — to stimulate economic activity in less-developed regions — when considered at a European level"[139].

Implications

All this raises "serious questions as to the rationale for pursuing policies that cannot be subject to proper evaluation"[140]. Bachtler *et al.*, nevertheless, conclude that "the Commission's control of incentives has been broadly effective in that it has resulted in a robust regulatory framework, recognised by Member States and backed by judicial review"[141]. The system of controls is thus perhaps best understood as a system of bounded competition, in which EU government subsidies to large investment projects (of which many, but not all, are foreign-owned) have been confined to designated areas by the controls exercised by the Commission, and limited in terms of the level of award rates and overall spending by the governments' own budget constraints.

The Commission itself claims success in having reduced the levels of government spending on incentives to attract FDI[142]. Clearly, on paper, the Commission's approach to disciplining incentives-based competition among EU governments provides the key elements it needs to ensure effective control. But, equally clearly, there are some weaknesses in the Commission's approach in practice.

One weakness is that while the Commission has effectively constrained the *spatial* coverage of EU governments' investment-incentives (and regional-aids) programmes over the last 20 years, it does not constrain the level of spending on FDI incentives. The question then becomes, does this matter, especially in view of the downward trend in spending?

Arguably the reason it matters most is that contrary to the avowed objective of regional-aids programmes, which is to give poorer regions and areas a competitive edge *vis-à-vis* more prosperous regions and areas in attracting large investment projects, investment-incentives programmes actually tend less to counterbalance than to reinforce existing differences in locational "attractiveness" within Europe. Countries authorised to offer the highest award rates tend precisely to be those that most lack the budget resources needed to do so. Portugal's per capita spending on regional aids is about one-tenth of Germany's, for example, and Ireland, Spain, Greece and Portugal all spend less per capita on investment incentives than the EU average even though their per capita incomes are also well below the EU average. As in the United States, there is thus little evidence that incentives competition is serving the cause of raising incomes and creating jobs in the poorest areas of Europe; the evidence rather suggests that the competition tends to favour the more prosperous countries.

Another weakness is that in seeking to monitor and discipline incentives competition among governments, the Commission addresses its requests for information and its Decisions on State aids to national governments. Increasingly, however, regional and local authorities deal directly with investors — notably in providing such incentives as workers' training programmes and site donation and preparation. National authorities often have little motivation to pursue sub-national governments in responding to the Commission's inquiries and Decisions. The growing importance of local and regional governments in incentives-based competition thus points up considerable scope for local and regional governments to evade the Commission's scrutiny.

A third weakness is the extent to which the Commission may ultimately lack the political independence, and thus the administrative authority, it needs *vis-à-vis* EU governments. While the powers of the Commission are considerable — "the Commission effectively combines the role of legislator, policeman, prosecutor and judge" *vis-à-vis* national governments in matters of state aids, matters in which the

Commission arguably has more power than in any other policy area[143] — the Commission's exercise of this power has in fact generated considerable controversy with member states (notably over defining the precise geographical boundaries of regions and areas qualifying for state aids), that controversy has subsided in recent years. Part of the reason it has subsided is that the Commission has shifted away from "drawing maps" and towards defining the proportion of a country's population eligible for regional assistance. An important part of the reason may also be some weakening in recent years in the Commission's ability to impose its views, as both France and Germany (notorious for their disputes with the Commission in this area) have been able to negotiate major increases in the population ceilings which the Commission intended to set, and then to designate the areas eligible for assistance largely on their own terms[144].

The greatest danger, however, may not be that of a weakened Commission in terms of its ability to discipline the use of state aids; indeed, award-rate ceilings already do not "bite" as noted earlier. Rather, it may be that the detailed nature of the Commission's involvement in (some would say micro-management of) governments' investment-incentives programmes via its control of state aids could induce governments increasingly to pursue less transparent means than grants to attract investors. Particularly worrisome in this regard is the danger of growing tax competition, since only a fraction of tax incentives to attract corporate investment are considered "State aids" and thus subject to control by the Commission[145].

Indeed, while state aids may be seen by some as little more than relatively expensive means to attract large investment projects, the advantage of capital grants in particular is that they are relatively transparent in the triple sense of being *i)* relatively visible and easy to understand for potential recipients; *ii)* flexible and easy to administer for governments; and *iii)* relatively easy to monitor and police for the Commission. In Central and Eastern Europe, on the other hand, as in the bulk of non-OECD countries, tax concessions have been more important than financial incentives in the competition to attract investment.

The danger of growing tax competition among EU governments has thus led the EU Council, in December 1997, to adopt a Code of Conduct for business taxation in which member states agree not to introduce "harmful" tax measures and to roll back existing harmful measures[146]. In November 1998, the Commission issued a notice on the application of state aid rules to measures relating to direct business taxation measures, committing itself as well to examine or re-examine all such measures in member states. Beyond reducing maximum incentive award-rates for EU governments' regional investment incentives policies (from 75 to 50 per cent of eligible investment costs in least-favoured regions and from 30 to 20 per cent of those costs in development areas), efforts are also being made to increase the coherence between individual EU governments' state aids programmes and the Commission's own regional-assistance programmes — paid for with "Structural Funds", these account for about one-third of the $100 billion EU budget — particularly in view of the expected eastern enlargement of the European Union in the coming years.

The achievements of the EU approach to disciplining governments' use of investment incentives and to addressing the "prisoner's dilemma" that makes it so difficult to rein-in incentives-based competition are thus considerable. As Bachtler *et al.* observe, it "provides a regulatory framework, some measure of autonomy for the supervisory body, and procedures for enforcement and sanctions that are backed by provisions for judicial review. All this adds up to a system of controlling subsidies that is unique in international law and finds no parallel even in individual countries with federal structures; for a Community of 15 sovereign states, this represents a considerable success in co-operation and policy co-ordination"[147].

Individual European national and sub-national governments are also increasingly giving attention to improving the attractiveness of their jurisdictions to investors by continuously upgrading both such "tangible" attractions as modern and well-performing telecommunications and transportation infrastructure, and such key "intangibles" as the availability of high-quality health and educational services. Both are needed to contribute to the development of the kind of highly creative and contact-rich environment that forward-looking investors often find most attractive. Rules-based competition in Europe, as discussed in Chapter 3, seems also to be working in this direction.

Competition in Canada[148]

With an inward FDI stock of some $137 billion, Canada hosts about one-fifth the amount of FDI stock in the United States (and accounts for 15 per cent of FDI stock in NAFTA countries, with Mexico accounting for another 8 per cent). That stock nevertheless corresponds to 22 per cent of Canada's GDP — as compared to ratios of about 21 per cent in Ireland and the United Kingdom, 13 per cent for the European Union as a whole, and 8 per cent in the United States — which points up the considerable importance of FDI for the Canadian economy[149]. More than two-thirds of that FDI is from the United States, 13 per cent is from countries in the European Union (8 per cent from the United Kingdom alone, the second largest source country) and 4 per cent is from Japan[150].

FDI Policy Liberalisation and Investment Incentives

Canada's policy stance on inward FDI has moved from one of relatively high levels of protection and discrimination against foreign investment in the 1960s and 1970s, to a more liberal and welcoming stance since 1984. Particularly noteworthy during the earlier period was the creation in 1974 of the Foreign Investment Review Agency, which was abolished in 1984. During its ten years of existence, FIRA examined some 6 300 foreign-investment applications. While it approved 90 per cent of those applications, one cannot know how many applications were simply never submitted in the context of an investment climate described by many observers at the time as "hostile" — a time during which FDI inflows fell from 13 to 2 per cent of total net financial inflows[151]. Many of Canada's ten provincial governments lamented the country's poor investment climate during this period as well[152].

Following the Conservative government's election in 1984, FIRA was abolished and in its place "Investment Canada" was created with a mandate to encourage and facilitate investment in Canada. Apparently more important to the liberalisation of Canada's policy stance on FDI over time, however, has been the signing of the Canada-United States Free Trade Agreement in 1988, followed by NAFTA, ratified in 1993, and the WTO agreements on TRIMs and on Subsidies and Compensatory Measures. The results of these agreements (including their "national treatment" and "most favoured nation" clauses) is that subsidies which are judged to be "specific" to (i.e. discriminate in favour of) particular firms or investment projects are subject to compensatory measures; *general* subsidies, on the other hand, are permitted "under condition they do not constitute means of arbitrary discrimination among investors". The principle of "national treatment", in particular, makes it difficult, both for Canada's federal government and for its provincial governments, to offer incentives that target foreign investors if the governments do not have the means or the will to offer the same incentives to local investors. The incentives they offer tend to be focused on the promotion of investment in R & D and new technologies, on economic development in poorer regions, and on protecting the environment.

Today, the federal government has four regional development programmes — covering the Atlantic region, the province of Quebec, northern Ontario, and western Canada — which target small and medium-size firms, not FDI, but which also seek "to increase Canada's share of international investment"[153]. All ten of Canada's provincial governments also have administrative structures to attract investors (agencies, bureaux or ministerial offices), as do many municipalities.

Total enterprise subsidies, to foreign and local investors combined, amounted to an estimated $11.6 billion, or 1.6 per cent of Canada's GDP, in 1993 — of which 49 per cent came from provincial governments, 40 per cent from the federal government, and 11 per cent from municipal governments[154]. The ratio of total enterprise subsidies to GDP (1.6 per cent in 1993) has fallen from 2.7 per cent in 1981 and 2.1 per cent in 1987, while provincial governments have more than doubled their subsidies, and municipalities have tripled theirs, over the same period. Thus, since 1981, there has been a simultaneous decline of enterprise subsidies as a share of GDP, and a shift in their financing away from the federal government (which provided 70 per cent of the total in 1981 and 56 per cent in 1987, as compared to 40 per cent in 1993) to greater financing by provincial governments (whose share has risen from 27 per cent in 1981 to 49 per cent in 1993) and by municipal governments (whose share has risen from 4 per cent to 11 per cent)[155].

Firms in two provinces alone receive more than half the total value of enterprise subsidies in Canada. Ontario, with 40 per cent of the country's GDP, accounts for 27 per cent; Quebec, with 23 per cent of GDP, hosts 25 per cent. The next largest hosts to enterprise subsidies are Alberta (18 per cent, with 11 per cent of GDP); British Colombia (9 per cent, with 13 per cent of GDP); Manitoba (6 per cent with 3 per cent of GDP); and Saskatchewan (7 per cent, with 3 per cent of GDP). The remaining provinces and territories combined account for 8 per cent of enterprise subsidies and for 7 per cent of GDP[156].

Another approximately $5 billion goes to enterprises in the form of special tax reductions and fiscal incentives. Data on the distribution of these incentives by province, which permit comparisons of figures on fiscal incentives per worker with those on GDP per worker, indicate that these incentives tend to benefit the richer provinces.

Finally, data on 23 individual investment projects in the province of Quebec during the period 1995-98 provide a basis for estimating the approximate cost of public incentives provided per job directly to be created by FDI. That cost ranges from only a few thousand dollars in some cases to over $300 000 in one case and over $500 000 in another. The average is $86 000 per job, or about $50 000 if the two highest figures are simply ignored as extreme. The value of the incentives ranges from 4 per cent to 77 per cent of the total estimated amount of investment (in Europe called the "award rate"), with the average at 24 per cent, or $15 million per investment project.

Implications

First, as in the United States and Europe, the evidence in Canada does not point to a progressive impact of regional development subsidies on the inter-provincial distribution of income. Second, it points to a significant degree of competition among provincial governments, and to competition with potential investment-location sites in the United States that is often as important as competition among sites within Canada, or more important. Third, it points to a shift in the supply of incentives away from the federal government towards provincial and, to a lesser degree, municipal governments. Fourth, it shows a significant *level* of enterprise subsidies and fiscal incentives — very much in accordance with the significance of FDI in the Canadian economy, although the incentives data do not distinguish between foreign and locally owned enterprise recipients — but fifth, and equally significantly, the evidence does *not* point to any significant upward *trend* over time in the total value of incentives provided. It shows, rather, some decline in the value of incentives as a share of GDP — during a period when FDI inflows have grown significantly.

Where Canada is unique, among OECD countries, is in its establishment of a Code of Conduct on Incentives among provincial governments, as part of its 1995 "Internal Trade Agreement" designed to reduce inter-provincial barriers to trade and investment. Under the Code, "each Party seeks to avoid engaging in bidding wars to attract investors ... "[157]. The effectiveness of the Code is nevertheless limited by the weakness of the overall Agreement, which requires unanimous agreement on all decisions, and by the fact that the Code allows provincial governments to increase their supply of incentives whenever foreign jurisdictions — notably including potential investment sites in the United States — are perceived as competitors[158]. The net result is difficult to predict, and, as André and Françoy Raynauld conclude, it is too early to assess the effectiveness of the Code[159].

Summing Up the Evidence

Overall, the evidence on incentives-based competition indicates that such competition is both intense and widespread. It appears to have grown in tandem with the current wave of globalisation and the extraordinary growth of FDI since the mid-1980s.

Governments in both OECD and non-OECD countries, at both the national and sub-national level, engage actively in this competition. Rough estimates of the "cost-per-job" of incentive packages point to similar orders of magnitude of the cost of incentives in OECD and non-OECD countries — at least for major investment projects in the automobile industry. The rising "cost-per-job" over the last two decades also suggests an *intensification* of incentives-based competition, certainly in this industry, during that period.

One difference between incentives-based competition in OECD countries and that in non-OECD countries according to the UNCTAD report is that governments in OECD countries rely more on financial than on fiscal incentives, whereas non-OECD governments rely more on fiscal than on financial incentives. This finding, however, appears to reflect the UNCTAD report's focus on the use of incentives mainly by *national* governments, with little attention given to competition by sub-national governments, and the fact that EU national governments tend to rely heavily on the use of capital grants, as encouraged by the European Commission's control on "State aids" to poorer regions in EU countries. Sub-national governments are nevertheless the main competitors for FDI in many OECD countries, including the United States and Canada, and these governments often rely heavily on fiscal incentives. Our study does not, therefore, confirm UNCTAD's conclusion that there is a notable difference between OECD and non-OECD governments' net relative propensities to rely on fiscal rather than financial incentives.

Nor is the evidence on the *intensification* of incentives-based competition unambiguous. While there can be little doubt that more governments are involved in that competition than 20 years ago, and that the overall "cost-per-job" of the typical incentives package has risen, the evidence above all suggests that incentives-based competition has grown and become more widespread as governments (both OECD and non-OECD) have moved in the course of the 1980s and 1990s to liberalise their domestic and international economic policy regimes. It is this global movement towards more liberal policies which appears *both* to have created a more favourable environment for FDI — to which the global supply of FDI has responded positively — *and* to have increased pressures on governments, worldwide, to enhance the competitiveness of their economies. ("Competitiveness" here refers both to the ability of local firms to compete on global markets, and to the ability of the local economy to attract and retain firms that are successful global competitors.)

The evidence does not, in other words, indicate that increasing incentives-based competition has been responsible, in any significant way, for the major increase in the global supply of FDI that has occurred since the mid-1980s. Rather, insofar as any direct causal relationship can be identified between the global intensification of incentives-based competition and the global increase in the supply of FDI, the relationship appears to work in the other direction: as the global move by governments to liberalise economic policies has facilitated and stimulated the global growth of FDI (along with increased global inter-firm competition and corporate restructuring), governments have intensified competition with one another in seeking to attract "their share" of increased global FDI flows.

This interpretation is further buttressed by the considerable evidence that most incentives-based competition involves governments' seeking to compete with neighbouring governments for investment that is already, in principle, destined for their country or region. Most of the competition is, in other words, intra-regional.

The evidence on the intensification of incentives-based competition is somewhat ambiguous in another sense as well: it does not establish any clear pattern of, or point to any inexorable tendency towards, unrestrained bidding wars among governments in their competition to attract major investment projects. Clearly, such "wars" can and do occur, and the prisoner's-dilemma nature of the competition creates a permanent danger in this regard. However, as the European experience indicates, such wars can be restrained, contained or avoided — whether it be, in the specific case of Europe, thanks to the limits established by the Treaty of Rome and imposed by the European Commission, thanks to the limits effectively imposed by the budget constraints that national governments face (and global financial markets now tend to reinforce), or both.

Hard evidence is also unfortunately lacking that would enable meaningful measurement of the costs and benefits of incentives. Part of the problem is the difficulty of obtaining data on the value, i.e. the direct cost to governments, of the incentives they actually provide to investors. Even in those cases where the cost of an incentives package is known, the difficulty of measuring the value of the benefits derived by the host economy from the investment attracted — not to mention the difficulty of knowing if the package was actually decisive in attracting the investment — adds to the difficulty of undertaking meaningful cost-benefit analyses of incentives programmes.

The evidence, in sum, provides no more than weak support for the negative-sum game interpretation of incentives-based competition. This conclusion is only strengthened by cases of relatively expensive incentives packages — such as that of the Mercedes investment in Alabama — where reasonable estimates of the package's costs and benefits fail to confirm that the package is likely to have a negative net return for the economy paying for it. Of course, the *distortionary* effects of incentives that discriminate among sectors and often against smaller firms, as well as among potential investment locations, may impose major additional economic costs — costs which may ultimately be greater than the direct fiscal and financial costs of incentives paid out — but it is unclear how much the costs of such distortions can be attributed to the effects of *competition* among governments to attract FDI, i.e. to the effects of incentives *per se,* and how much should be attributed, on the contrary, to governments' desire to be *selective* in their FDI targeting efforts, and/or to their desire to influence the impact (e.g. on exports) of whatever FDI comes in. Moreover, the same move towards more open and liberal policy regimes that tends to stimulate competition among governments to attract FDI, combined with the importance that investors attach to choosing sites with sound fundamentals before they allow incentives to influence their location decisions, tends to limit the degree of market distortions — and thus to limit the economic costs associated with those distortions — actually caused by incentives.

On the other hand, the evidence does not provide more than weak support for the positive-sum game interpretation of incentives-based competition. First, while the competition may induce governments to devote some additional effort and resources to the enhancement of local supplies of human capital and infrastructure, compared to what they would have devoted in the absence of such competition — as is consistent with the positive-sum game hypothesis — the evidence suggests that the additional resources actually devoted to such enhancement that is induced by competition to attract FDI is but a small proportion of the total value of most incentive packages. One cannot, in other words, reject the hypothesis that incentives ultimately tend more to compete with, than to augment, the use of public resources to increase local supplies of productivity-enhancing human-capital formation and modern infrastructure. Secondly, as noted previously, the evidence does not support the hypothesis that intensifying competition among governments to attract FDI is responsible for increasing the global supply of FDI.

The evidence also suggests that while governments often "justify" their provision of investment incentives on the grounds that the incentives are needed to steer investment to poorer areas within a country, in actual practice the incentives are of limited effectiveness in this regard, and sometimes actually reinforce inequalities instead. The evidence suggests as well that while most governments make no nominal distinction between foreign and domestic investors in their investment-incentives programmes, the focus of many of those programmes on targeting large or more technology-intensive investments means that the incentives programmes tend, in actual practice, to be geared towards attracting FDI.

The single greatest cost of incentives-based competition may thus be the lack of transparency that tends to be associated with incentives programmes. While both the governments that supply incentives and the investors that receive them have reasons not to reveal the details of actual incentives packages — governments because of a desire to escape a "ratcheting up" of incentives and to avoid "bidding wars" insofar as possible, investors because of a desire to protect confidential business information (e.g. on costs) from competitors — this lack of transparency makes incentives-based competition particularly vulnerable to graft, corruption and other (even legal) rent-seeking behaviour that can be highly destructive both to the development of competitive markets and to the development of a modern state and accountable government. For policy makers in developing and emerging economies, this danger, and the prisoner's-dilemma nature of incentives-based competition, point to the importance of *i)* closely monitoring their own use of incentives; *ii)* working with other national governments, on a regional basis and/or in a multilateral framework, to monitor the use of incentives and limit the negative effects of incentives-based competition, and *iii)* moving away from incentives-based competition towards greater reliance on *rules-based* means of competing to attract FDI.

Table 2.1. **Investment Incentives in the Automobile Industry**

Date of Package	Country of Project	Investor	Amount per Job* (US dollars)
1980	United States	Honda	4 000
early 1980s	United States	Nissan	17 000
1984	United States	Mazda-Ford	14 000
mid-1980s	United States	GM Saturn	27 000
mid-1980s	United States	Mitsubishi-Chrysler	35 000
mid-1980s	United States	Toyota	50 000
mid-1980s	United States	Fuji-Isuzu	51 000
early 1990s	United States	Mercedes Benz	168 000
1992	Portugal	Ford-Volkswagen	265 000
1995	Brazil	Volkswagen	54 000-94 000
1996	Brazil	Renault	133 000
1996	Brazil	Mercedes Benz	340 000
1997	Germany	Volkswagen	180 000
1997	India	Ford	200 000-420 000

Note*:   Estimated value of fiscal and financial incentives supplied by national and sub-national governments to a particular investment project, divided by the number of jobs the project was expected directly to create.

Sources: Unofficial, cited in Donahue (United States), Bachtler *et al.* (Europe), Da Motta Veiga and Iglesias (Brazil) and Venkatesan *et al.* (India).

Notes

1. UNCTAD (1996).

2. See OECD (1998).

3. The same applies to the "transition" economies in Central and Eastern Europe where, in addition, tax stabilisation regimes (freezing the fiscal regime for a specific investment project for an extended period) have been offered as a guarantee against frequent fluctuations of the fiscal regime.

4. UNCTAD (1996), pp. 37-39.

5. UNCTAD (1996), p. 76.

6. This section draws heavily from Da Motta Veiga and Iglesias (1998).

7. UNCTAD (1998). The data on FDI:GDP ratios are for 1996.

8. At end-1985, Brazil's stock of inward FDI was about $26 billion and that of China less than $4 billion. Average annual FDI inflows in 1985-90 were about $1.3 billion in Brazil and $2.6 billion in China (UNCTAD, 1997).

9. Referring to this period, Da Motta Veiga and Iglesias observe that "in reality the Federal Government co-administered the geographical allocation of new investments" (Da Motta Veiga and Iglesias, 1998, p. 12).

10. A number of states did in fact begin to seek more actively to attract "their share" of the booming flow of FDI into Brazil in the early 1970s, notably by offering tax concessions and tax holidays to investors. The major beneficiary of that flow, the state of São Paulo, then successfully pressured the Federal Government in 1975 to enact a law (CLD 24/75) explicitly restricting the autonomy of Brazil's sub-national governments to pursue that activity. This law still exists, but, as explained below, is not enforced.

11. Da Motta Veiga and Iglesias (1998), p. 15.

12. *Ibid.*

13. *Ibid*, p. 20.

14. *Ibid*, Table 5, p. 69.

15. Some packages also include state participation in a project's equity — directly or via a public development fund — not so much as a financial incentive, at least for large investors with easy access to funding, but as a means to formalise the government's commitment to the success of the project and thus serve to mitigate political risk.

16. Da Motta Veiga and Iglesias, *ibid*, Box 2, pp. 55-56. The authors stress that the estimates are crude, and that "no assessment of cost/benefit ratios is being made".

17. *Ibid*.

18. *Ibid*, p. 27.

19. *Ibid*, p. 29.

20. A partial caveat concerns the projects announced for the poorer northern regions: these projects had to be registered by end-May 1997 in order to benefit from the special incentives available under the Auto Regime, but many are not expected to come to fruition.

21. *Ibid*, p. 46.

22. *Ibid*, p. 5.

23. *Ibid*, p. 22.

24. Nor, indeed, does the federal government's tolerance of sub-national governments' use of fiscal incentives to attract investment impede the government from exercising considerable pressure on state governments to limit their debts and reduce their fiscal deficits (see Da Motta Veiga and Iglesias, pp. 20-21).

25. *Ibid*, p. 61.

26. *Ibid*, p. 60.

27. *Ibid*, pp. 60-61.

28. *Ibid*, p. 62.

29. *Ibid*, p. 62.

30. This section draws heavily on Campos (1998).

31. UNCTAD (1998), *op. cit.*

32. Argentina's stabilisation plan is called the "Convertibility Plan" because of the government's commitment to convert one Argentinean currency unit into one US dollar, on demand.

33. Campos explains that Argentina's provincial governments' main source of tax revenue is a type of income tax that cannot exceed 3 per cent of a firm's sales and which, moreover, "has been abolished in most provinces for [firms in] a variety of sectors as part of a deal with the national government [in which] the latter agreed to reduce the 'social charges' on wages for firms in sectors where the provinces decided not to charge their income tax" (Campos, 1998, p. 40).

34. *Ibid.*, p. 21.

35. *Ibid*, p. 18. The author also cites Under-secretary of Mining estimates that about 20 000 direct jobs and 82 000 indirect jobs will be created in the mining industry by the year 2000.

36. The new royalty has in fact generated some tension between investors and the government of the Province of Catamarca over the question of how to determine the value of production that should serve as the basis for calculating the royalty, with the provincial government taking the position that it should be the gross value of output and investors arguing it should be the value net of production costs; this tension does not, therefore, point to a danger of escalating incentives (Campos, 1998, p. 24). See also Mandel-Campbell, (1998, p. 34).

37. For a discussion of the role of flexible post-taylorist "lean" methods of work organisation in driving the current wave of globalisation, see Oman (1994 and 1996*a*).

38. As in Brazil, Argentina's auto parts producers — mostly domestic firms that developed during the import-substitution period — are suffering under the new auto regime. On the question of the relative importance of Mercosur and the stabilisation programme, Campos cites interview results suggesting that little FDI would have been forthcoming in this sector because of the successful stabilisation programme alone, whereas much FDI would probably have been forthcoming with the establishment of Mercosur even in the absence of the stabilisation programme. He also notes the importance of automakers' estimates that middle-income developing countries' demand growth for cars will be double that of the developed countries over the coming decade, and their perception of the importance of being present as producers in those markets to defend or increase their share of world auto markets. (Campos, 1998, p. 28).

39. *Ibid.*, p. 41.

40. See Chudnovsky, López and Porta (1997).

41. Campos (1998, p. 42).

42. *Ibid*, p. 9.

43. This section draws heavily from Sieh Lee (1988).

44. UNCTAD (1997 and 1998). The ratios of inward FDI stock to GDP are for 1996 (Annex Table B.6).

45. See Tan and Kulasingham *in* Oman (1984).

46. Sieh Lee, *op.cit.,* p. 4.

47. *Ibid.*

48. *Ibid*, p. 1.

49. *Ibid*, p. 40.

50. UNCTAD, *World Investment Report 1997*, reports that manufactured exports rose from 21 per cent of Malaysia's total exports in 1980 to 80 per cent in 1995, that two-thirds of manufactured exports (52 per cent of total exports) are electrical and electronics goods, that foreign affiliates account for the bulk of manufactured exports, and that 78 per cent of the inputs that go into exports are imported. That report also notes the negative contribution of FDI to Malaysia's trade balance: "With profit

remittances and other direct investment income payments averaging $2.8 billion per year, foreign affiliates had large current-account deficits during the period, generally surpassing the deficits registered for the country as a whole [while] local firms ... contributed positively to the current account" (p. 91).

51. Announced in 1995, the MSC project aims to propel the economy into the information age and productivity-growth-led economic growth by attracting and developing world-leading companies through "smart partnerships" between foreign and Malaysian firms in seven "Flagship Application" areas: smart schools, telemedicine, multipurpose smart cards, borderless marketing, R&D clusters, worldwide manufacturing web, and electronic government. To attract investors the Malaysian government plans to supply basic infrastructure (optic fibre networks, roads and rail links, etc.) at considerable expense — though it claims the bulk of investment costs will be borne by firms locating in the Corridor — and will offer incentives "far superior to those conventionally available to draw FDI" (Sieh Lee, 1998 p. 23). By April 1998, 124 companies had MSC status, including British Telecom, Fujitsu-ICL, DHL, NCR, NEC, Nippon T&T, Mitsubishi, Siemens, Reuters, Sumitomo, Sharp and Sun Microsystems — many having already bought land in the 750 km^2 Corridor for their R&D centres. As Sieh observes, the MSC project "is certainly innovative, brave and costly. [While] the cost of failure [also] has to be taken into account ... the risk of failure has to be matched against the cost of facing the economic consequences of a much reduced FDI inflow as competition for it intensifies" (*ibid.*, p. 24).

52. Sieh Lee, *ibid.,* pp. 5-6.

53. *Ibid.*, p. 9.

54. *Ibid.*, p. 8.

55. *Ibid.*, pp. 28-29.

56. *Ibid.*

57. *Ibid.*

58. *Ibid.*, p. 37.

59. This section draws heavily on Chia (1998).

60. UNCTAD (1997). The data refer to 1995. The handful of countries which appear to have higher ratios — Vanuatu, several small Caribbean islands, Liberia and Swaziland — are tax havens whose FDI stock exists largely on paper only.

61. Chia (1998), pp. 19, 21.

62. Singapore's population of about 3 million is less than 1 per cent of the ASEAN countries' combined population of about 435 million. (UNCTAD, 1997, provides data on FDI stocks and flows.)

63. See Pang Eng Fong (1984) and Oman (1984a).

64. In the 1960-65 period, net capital inflows were almost four times the level of domestic savings and financed almost 80 per cent of domestic investment (Chia, 1998, p. 7).

65. In the 1980-85 period, net capital inflows were one-seventh the level of domestic savings and financed about 12 per cent of domestic investment. From 1986 onwards, domestic savings exceeded investment and Singapore became a net capital exporter. However, much of Singapore's large domestic savings is controlled by the government (compulsory savings under the Central Provident Fund and public-sector surpluses) and is not readily available for private-sector manufacturing investments. Much of it has gone into the build-up of foreign reserves and the construction of housing and physical infrastructure.

66. UNCTAD (1997), p. 87.

67. Chia (1998), p. 5.

68. *Ibid*, p. 6.

69. *Ibid*, p. 14.

70. *Ibid*, p. 12.

71. This section draws heavily on Hu Angang (1998) and Chen (1998).

72. UNCTAD (1998).

73. See for example, ILO (1998*b*).

74. In May to November of 1997, Edward Chen interviewed six government officials and six corporate managers in Shenzhen, and similar numbers both in the Xiamen Special Economic Zone in Fujian Province, and in Dalian City in Liaoning Province.

75. This section draws heavily on Venkatesan *et al.* (1998).

76. UNCTAD (1998).

77. *Ibid*.

78. World Bank (1997).

79. Venkatesan *et al.* (1998).

80. The index ranged from a minimum of 13 in Punjab to a maximum of 133 in Himachal Pradesh, with the index in 11 out of 16 states falling between 50 and 100; only in 3 states was the index below 50 and only in two was it above 100. The co-efficient of variation of the index among the 16 states also declined between the two periods.

81. Of the five states selected for more detailed study, two states (Maharashtra and Uttar Pradesh) showed an increase in their incentives index between the two periods, one state (Gujarat) showed a small decline, and two states (Tamil Nadu and Haryana) showed no change.

82. Venkatesan *et al.* (1998), p. 61.

83. *Ibid*.

84. The regression model explains "only" about half the variation in the investment variable because it does not consider the influence of such factors as local political conditions, labour problems and the presence of agglomeration economies. The regression co-efficient of the infrastructure index (67.04) is much higher than the co-efficient of the incentives index (00.50).

85. Venkatesan *et al.* (1998), p. 72.

86. Venkatesan *et al.* (1998), p. 79.

87. *Ibid.*

88. The 12 per cent rate of discount is used by Venkatesan *et al.* in their social benefit/ cost analysis of the incentives provided for this project, as referred to in the text below. In estimating the benefits from the investment project, they assume an employment multiplier effect of 6, an investment multiplier effect of 2.5, and a 25 per cent premium on foreign exchange.

89. Venkatesan *et al.* (1998), pp. 93-94.

90. See note 88.

91. Venkatesan *et al.* (1998), p. 120.

92. The data are from UNCTAD (1997, 1998).

93. This discussion of incentives-based competition in the United States draws heavily on Donahue (1998).

94. Thus, whereas in the 1960s, US companies invested abroad about 8 dollars for each dollar invested by non-US firms in the United States, in the 1980s they invested abroad about 57 cents for each dollar invested by non-US firms in the U.S. The sources of FDI inflows into the United States are mainly EU countries (over two-thirds), Japan (16 per cent) and Canada (8 per cent).

95. For a discussion of the microeconomic forces that drive globalisation, including FDI, and a comparison of the current and past waves of globalisation, see Oman (1994 and 1996*a*).

96. Donahue (1998), p. 2.

97. The words are those of the Director of KPMG Peat Marwick business incentives group, as quoted by Donahue (1998), p. 11, from Johnston (1995).

98. Bartik (1994), reported in Donahue (1998), p. 11.

99. The number of states offering R&D tax incentives rose from 9 in 1977 to 36 in 1996; the number offering property-tax exemptions rose from 23 to 37; the number offering revenue bond financing rose from 20 to 44; the number offering construction finance assistance rose from 19 to 42; those offering equipment and machinery loans rose from 13 to 43, and equipment and machinery loan *guarantees* from 13 to 30; and those offering corporate income tax exemptions rose from 21 to 37.

100. The average rose from 11 in 1975 to 24 in 1995.

101. KPMG Peat Marwick LLP, Business Incentives Group (1995).

102. The plants are those of Volkswagen in Pennsylvania (closed ten years later); Honda in Ohio (1980: 5 300 jobs, about $4 000 per job); Nissan in Tennessee (4 000 jobs, $17 000 per job); Mazda-Ford in Michigan (1984: $14 000 per job); Saturn (GM) in Tennessee (mid-1980s: 3 000 jobs, $27 000 per job); Mitsubishi-Chrysler in Illinois (mid-1980s: over $35 000 per job); Toyota in Kentucky (mid-1980s: about $50 000

per job); Fuji-Isuzu in Indiana (mid-1980s: about $51 000 per job); BMW in South Carolina (1992: about $70 000 per job); Daimler-Benz in Alabama ($168 000 per job). As reported in Donahue, *op. cit.*, pp. 15-19.

103. Regarding the distinction between domestic and foreign investors, and its relative insignificance for our purposes, Donahue argues that, "Foreign-based firms could differ consistently from US-based firms — offering better jobs, or worse jobs; delivering collateral benefits in the form of new technologies, management approaches, global linkages, or imposing hidden costs on the US economy. But while there are ample anecdotes ... there are few systematic distinguishing features of foreign firms, beyond the obvious observations that weak firms seldom expand internationally, and that corporations tend to carry elements of their home country's business culture with them" (p. 14). Donahue also notes that for much of its sovereign history, "the United States has been a major recipient of foreign investment, with outward FDI only surpassing inward investment in the latter half of the 20th century".

104. The idea is that the interaction of supply (by states) and demand (by firms) in the "market" for investment sites will lead, over time, either to the development and dissemination of more efficient approaches *per se*, and to heterogeneous groups of states and firms "sorting themselves out" to find the best "fit" between individual states and individual investment projects.

105. Mowry (1990).

106. Donahue (1998).

107. *Ibid.*, p. 32.

108. In addition to the view of politicians as cynically willing to exploit popular credulity about their ability to "create jobs", cited earlier, other reasons why many state politicians persisted to act as if they could influence business location decisions, despite all the evidence to the contrary, were thought to include: politicians may be complicit with business interests eager for subsidies and tax breaks; politicians may be sceptical about the effectiveness of incentives but are unwilling to abandon such policies and risk the consequences of being wrong; some politicians may simply ignore the evidence, or be too dim to grasp it.

109. Donahue (1998), p. 29.

110. *Ibid.*, pp. 33-34.

111. *Ibid.*, p. 34.

112. *Ibid.* See also Peters and Fisher (1997).

113. Donahue (1998), p. 36.

114. Krugman and Graham (1989), p. 119.

115. See Donahue (1998), p. 38. The Supreme Court found in 1985 that "a State's goal of bringing in new business is legitimate and often admirable," and in 1994 that a "pure subsidy funded out of general revenues ordinarily imposes no burden on interstate commerce, but merely assists local business".

116. *Ibid*, p. 37.

117. See, however, Fisher and Peters (1998).

118. This section draws heavily on Bachtler *et al.* (1998).

119. The data on FDI stocks in relation to GDP refer to 1996 GDP and are taken from Table B.6 in UNCTAD (1998).

120. The European Economic Community technically still exists as part of the European Union (Economic and Monetary Union) created by the Maastricht Accords of 1992.

121. As the European Council noted in 1971, in its Resolution on General Systems of Regional Aid, " ... one of the objectives of the co-ordination and adaptation of general systems of regional aid is to put an end to the outbidding between Member States in order to attract investments to their respective territories ... " (cited in Bachtler *et al.*, p. 73). Thus, as Bachtler *et al.* note, "since the 1960s, the issue of competition for mobile investment has been the driving force behind the development of Commission policy in controlling general investment aid and, in particular, regional aid" (p. 73).

122. Commission of the European Communities (1998), p. 3, fn. 11.

123. Data comparing award rates on incentives offered to foreign-owned investment projects with those on incentives offered to domestically owned projects in Great Britain during the period 1984-95 show consistently higher award rates for FDI projects. They also show the average size of FDI projects to have risen from 8.4 times the average size of domestic projects in 1984-86, to 10.4 times in 1993-95, i.e. not only are FDI projects on average much larger than domestic projects, the differential has grown. See Bachtler *et al.* (1998), Table 3.1, p. 55.

123. Bachtler *et al.* (1998), p. 52. "Greenfield investment is investment to create new capacity, as distinct from acquisitions".

125. *Ibid*, p. 28. The authors emphasise that the main focus of the efforts of FDI-promotion agencies in Western Europe is "competition with neighbouring countries and regions in Western Europe, rather than with other parts of the world. Agencies tend to design their promotional policies to attract projects that are already destined for Western Europe ... ".

126. *Ibid*, p. 66. The authors also report that in Hyundai's final site selection from among four shortlisted candidates, of which one was in Ireland and three in the United Kingdom, the large UK offer was decisive in eliminating the Irish candidate.

127. Examples supplied by Raines and Wishlade, co-authors in Bachtler *et al.* They emphasise that the figures are from "anecdotal accounts in press reports" and that "the figures by no means represent total aid provided to the firms, just the main incentive grants (and only those offered, not necessarily those paid out)".

128. Commission of the European Communities (1996).

129. Bachtler *et al.*, Chapter 5. The authors further note that tax incentives constitute about a third of "State aids", in value terms, according to data for 1990-92. They also explain, however, that narrowly defined "tax incentives" represent only a fraction of OECD-defined "tax expenditures" (i.e. foregone tax revenues) involved in tax competition (the latter are some 15 times the value of the former) and that it

is important to distinguish between discriminatory "tax incentives" and non-discriminatory "tax advantages" and "tax systems". A good example of the latter is Ireland's 10 per cent corporate tax rate in manufacturing, designed specifically to attract direct corporate investment — apparently rather successfully — which prior to July 1998 was not subject to EC control as "State aids" because it was considered broad and therefore non-discriminatory. Another important example is social security: a relatively low level of obligatory social security contributions may be a powerful attraction to FDI highlighted by promotion agencies, but there is little evidence of manipulation of the level of obligatory contributions to attract FDI (and social security taxes do constitute an important part of the overall tax burden).

130. *Ibid*, p. 65.

131. *Ibid*, Tables 3.1 and 3.4.

132. *Ibid*, Table 3.6. The figures are in constant (1993) $US at PPP exchange rates.

133. *Ibid*, Figure 3.1.

134. *Ibid*, p. 67.

135. *Ibid*, pp. 76-77.

136. *Ibid*, p. 139. Elsewhere the authors note, quite appropriately, that: "What investors consider the most important locational factors is not necessarily what is the determining factor in practice. Hence, the final selection of the site has often depended largely on the financial package offered by the region or country" (*ibid*, p. 57). Some investors have even been known to draw-up their shortlist of preferred sites using maps of available incentives, before entering negotiations to determine their final site selection (*ibid*, p. 57).

137. *Ibid*, p. 57.

138. *Ibid*, p. 59.

139. *Ibid*, p. 139.

140. *Ibid*, p. 67.

141. *Ibid*, p. 136.

142. *Ibid*, p. 83.

143. Bachtler *et al.*, pp. 70-71. Control of State aids is also one of the few policy areas in which the Commission can act independently of the EU Council of Ministers.

144. *Ibid*, p. 76.

145. Tax incentives, as distinct from capital grants and other "financial" incentives, currently constitute about one-third of recorded "State aids" as mentioned earlier in note 129. See also the discussion in that note on the important conceptual distinction between tax "incentives" and broader tax "advantages" or even tax "systems" used to attract FDI.

146. A Council group is examining potentially harmful measures to determine if they fall under the Code. See also OECD (1998).

147. Bachtler *et al.*, p. 87.

148. This section draws heavily on A. and F. Raynauld (1998).

149. Data are from UNCTAD (1998).

150. A. and F. Raynauld (1998).

151. Drouin and Bruce-Briggs (1978).

152. *Ibid.*

153. Raynauld and Raynauld (1998), p. 98.

154. *Ibid.*, Table 4.1

155. *Ibid.*

156. *Ibid.*, Table 4.2.

157. *Ibid*, p. 66.

158. *Ibid.*, p 114.

159. *Ibid.*, p. 71.

Chapter 3

Rules-based Competition

Rules-based forms of competition by governments to attract FDI constitute a more disparate group of phenomena than do incentives-based forms, as noted in Chapter 1. Two rules-based forms that have generated particular controversy in recent years, notably in debates over the effects of "globalisation", stem from the role of government regulations and legal standards in the protection of the environment, on the one hand, and in the defence of workers' rights and the establishment of minimum labour standards, on the other. The concern, expressed by many, is that in competing to attract FDI, governments may overtly or covertly relax their enforcement of those standards — on a *de facto* if not on a *de jure* basis — thereby putting pressure on other governments to follow suit. The predicted result is growing downward pressure on those standards worldwide, analogous to the upward pressure on incentives, where governments are caught in a prisoner's dilemma and thus find it increasingly difficult to resist that pressure.

The milder version of this concern is that, over time, governments will fail to raise those standards to the degree, or at the speed, they would have done in the absence of unbridled policy competition for investment. Stronger versions evoke images of "a race to the bottom" caused by regulatory competition that is reminiscent of the inter-war process of competitive currency devaluations — with perhaps even worse consequences in the current era of globalisation. Advocates of this interpretation decry "social dumping" and "pollution havens".

This chapter looks first at the evidence on these two highly controversial forms of rules-based competition. It then looks at several very different — and generally much more effective — rules-based policy means to attract FDI, including international regional integration agreements, privatisation of state-owned enterprises, enhanced protection of intellectual property rights, improved government accountability and strengthened judiciary systems.

Environmental Standards

Few policy issues have generated more heated debate — and arguably less empirical clarity — than the "pollution haven" debate. What limited evidence exists provides scant support for the "race to the bottom" hypothesis. It suggests *i)* that firms in modern manufacturing and service industries rarely move their operations to take advantage of lower environmental standards in another country; and *ii)* that efforts by national governments to compete for FDI in these industries through lax standards or lax enforcement of environmental protection are likely to be unsuccessful, perhaps even counterproductive.

The "pollution haven" hypothesis first became an international issue in the late 1970s, following a wave of US legislation that shifted jurisdiction for many decisions on pollution control in the United States from the states to the federal government. The new federal laws, some Americans argued, could cause a massive relocation of industry to "pollution havens" in developing countries[1]. Subsequent studies have nevertheless found little evidence of US firms, or other OECD-based firms, closing and moving because of high environmental regulation costs. The reason is essentially that the costs of complying with anti-pollution laws have turned out to be relatively modest, on the whole, and any lure of weak environmental rules is simply swamped, in most cases, by other factors[2]. Studies have also pointed out that the bulk of OECD countries' outward FDI — including in most "dirty" industries[3] — goes to other highly-regulated OECD countries rather than to developing countries[4].

Significant exceptions to this general pattern, i.e. cases where companies have actually dismantled production facilities in OECD countries and moved them to lower-standard developing countries, appear not only to be few in number, but often to involve *sales* of outdated equipment to undercapitalised firms in fast-growing developing countries. Town and village enterprises in rural China, for example, have been known to purchase high-polluting used equipment because it is cheap[5].

Many of the worst examples of this type of "technology dumping" also reportedly involve non-OECD suppliers or investors[6]. Where OECD-based investors are involved, the investment projects are often natural-resource-seeking FDI in *undifferentiated* products for which demand is highly price-elastic. Examples have been reported in mining, fisheries, forestry and pulp, plantation crops and petroleum refining[7]. For these projects, small cost differences can translate into large market-share effects, and investment profitability is particularly susceptible to cost differences — including those of protecting the environment.

Even in the resource industries, moreover, the trend now is for major investors to seek less to take advantage of potentially weaker standards of environmental protection in developing countries. An important reason is the imposition of higher environmental standards by global investors' home countries and by the multilateral lending institutions. For example, the US Ex-Im Bank requires borrowers to meet its environmental guidelines, and the US Overseas Private Investment Corporation requires environmental impact assessments from US companies seeking political risk insurance for overseas projects (insurance that is particularly important in large resource-based projects in developing countries). OPIC also requires environmental management plans on all projects that it supports in developing countries — including annual reporting by the project developers on their environmental performance. The World Bank Group, including the International Finance Corporation, and the regional development banks are also laying down more stringent environmental performance requirements for projects they finance.

Numerous studies have also found that large investors tend to apply a world-wide environmental standard to all of their operations, thereby resulting in some "levelling-up" of pollution-control technologies across countries. Reasons why they tend to apply a global standard include the fact that it is often more efficient to run a single set of environmental practices worldwide than to scale-back practices at a single location; the high local visibility of large multinational investors can make them particularly attractive targets for local enforcement officials; and the memory of such events as the Bhopal disaster, in India, and the ensuing problems faced by Union Carbide, have heightened many investors' awareness of their potential environmental liabilities when they invest abroad[8]. UNCTAD's highly comprehensive study of multinational corporations' environmental performance also found that larger firms are more likely to have well-established environmental management systems and better environmental performance, which it attributed to economies of scale in production and administration; it also found that environmental management practices are strongly affected by conditions in the investor's country of origin, especially when the investment project is in a developing country[9].

FDI can also have positive knock-on or spillover effects on local firms in developing countries. One reason, of growing importance as technologically more demanding "flexible" or "just-in-time" systems of manufacturing organisation take root and spread in developing economies, is that by demanding particular quality standards, and providing the technical assistance needed to meet them, major foreign manufacturers can help local suppliers greatly to improve their overall efficiency; a corollary effect is often to improve their environmental performance as wastage is greatly reduced[10]. Another reason is that local firms will often try to imitate foreign investors' technological practices ("reverse engineering") and further spillovers occur as local firms employ staff previously employed by foreign investors. Privatisation of formerly inefficient state-owned-enterprises can also subject those enterprises to higher environmental standards when major foreign investors subject to stockholder pressures in their home countries are involved[11].

Rather ironically, there is more evidence that governments have tended to refrain from enforcing higher standards of environmental protection out of *fear* that their firms would suffer a competitive disadvantage, than there is evidence of firms actually relocating to take advantage of lower environmental standards in other countries. Studies of German firms, for example, similar to those of US firms cited earlier, have shown that most firms want to stay near their major markets and tend to develop higher-standard technologies, which they often subsequently install in their affiliates in developing countries, rather than moving to lower-standard countries. But many also have admitted to *threatening* to relocate when negotiating their siting decisions with their government[12].

Another illustration is that of a major Dutch chemical company which threatened to relocate to a nearby country unless the government agreed to make concessions on environmental standards. As Bachtler *et al.* observe, "When the Dutch government refused to concede, there were no further developments — the company had been bluffing, but it would readily have accepted relaxed regulations"[13].

Enhanced international policy co-operation on environmental standards may thus be desirable, less as a means to counteract actual "pollution haven" competition among governments or industrial relocation to lower-standard countries, than as a means to contain the downward pressure on environmental standards caused by governments' fear of such competition. The argument for policy co-operation on environmental standards is only reinforced, of course, by the free-rider problem in the case of pollution or environmental problems that span national boundaries, i.e. in cases where some of those who would share in the benefits of environmental quality improvements do not have to share in the costs of those improvements. Sovereignty considerations, which make it difficult for one country to influence the environmental behaviour of another, constitute a further reason for such co-operation[14].

Positive Effects

The story does not, however, end here. More surprising perhaps — and certainly encouraging — one also finds evidence that points in the opposite direction from the "pollution haven" hypothesis. It suggests that competition among governments to attract corporate investment can, and in a growing number of cases does, create *upward* pressure on environmental standards. An important reason is the growing prevalence of relatively "clean" knowledge-intensive industries and services among those activities in which governments most actively seek to attract investment, combined with the growing desire of corporations investing in these activities to locate in communities where their managers and employees — and their productivity levels — will benefit from high standards of environmental protection.

Many firms are indeed discovering that locating in a community with high standards of environmental protection can increase their economic competitiveness. It does so via reduced operating costs (e.g. water filtration costs, worker-health problems, risks of incurring clean-up costs) as well as the attraction of high-quality human resources, and via the increased revenues that selling to increasingly environmentally-conscious markets can bring. The spillover benefits of "clustering" and "agglomeration economies" can in turn act as a powerful attraction to other corporate investors, thereby amplifying the investment- and FDI-attractiveness of communities, and economies, that enforce relatively high standards of environmental protection.

Thus, for example, while the Mexican government has significantly increased its environmental enforcement efforts in recent years, FDI in the Mexico City area has expanded rapidly at the same time as air quality (a major problem for years) has actually improved. A recent survey of multinational corporate investors in Mexico found that many of them feel that *reduced* government subsidies for power and water along with *more consistent enforcement* of existing pollution-control requirements would be the most effective ways for the government to improve firms' environmental performance[15]. In a similar vein, recent studies have found, in developing as well as in OECD countries, that companies are reporting more benefits than problems from investing in cleaner production; the reasons range from pressure exercised by customers, a commitment to corporate responsibility and anticipation of regulatory demands, to cost savings associated with greater process efficiency and increased competitiveness[16]. For a growing number of companies, "clean production" which seeks to design-out pollution problems, rather than deal with unwanted waste, is a way to design-in efficiency of raw material use as well as to reduce clean-up costs while minimising the environmental impact of production.

One study has also looked into the question of whether more liberal trade and investment policies are associated with more pollution-intensive industrialisation in developing countries. Focusing on Latin America, it found evidence that, over the 1970s and 1980s, the more open national economies ended up with cleaner production than did the more protectionist ones. While pollution intensity did grow more rapidly in the region as a whole after environmental regulations became stricter in OECD countries, in the more open countries of the region pressures grew in parallel for more stringent environmental standards, whereas pollution intensity grew in the protectionist countries. As one of the authors wrote in a companion piece, "Restrictive trade policies...may even have been the main stimulus to toxic industrial migration, rather than regulatory cost differences between the North and the South"[17].

Today, in any case, the notion of a trade-off between economic growth and competitiveness, on the one hand, and protection of the environment, on the other, is being replaced — in policy circles but also in many corporations — by one of progress towards sustainable development, in which higher standards of protection of the environment feature not as a deterrent but as an attraction to major investment projects. As Bachtler *et al.*, observe in their analysis of the effects of policy competition to attract FDI in Europe, "Current competitive drives to promote European locations as destinations for investment identify environmental advantages ranging from the quality of life and proximity to attractive landscapes ... to clear business advantages of being located in a country or region with high environmental standards and strict regulations. The latter can include: eco-audit and eco-labelling registrations being presented as business catalysts; recycling and energy efficiency being shown to bring financial benefits; and supply-chain linkages characterised by supplier and customer environmental audits which go beyond minimum compliance to be in advance of legislation or ahead of targets"[18]. Their conclusion is unambiguous: "Policy competition has *raised* standards [of environmental protection] across much of Europe"[19].

The policy challenge is reasonably clear: Governments must not cede to fears of competition from "pollution havens"; they must pursue, and enforce, environmental standards that work in favour of sustainable development. Companies should work with governments in that endeavour — internationally, nationally, locally — in developing and in OECD countries. International environmental policy co-ordination is highly desirable as well (especially, but not only, to protect the "global commons", as in the control of greenhouse gas emissions and protection of the ozone layer). Insofar as competition among governments to attract FDI acts as a hindrance to such policy co-ordination, it may deter a socially optimal *raising* of environmental standards; and there can be no doubt of the potential benefits from greater international environmental policy co-ordination[20]. Enhanced international policy co-ordination to limit the negative effects of competition for FDI on environmental standards is therefore desirable.

Labour Standards and Export-processing Zones

The debate over labour standards is not unlike that over environmental standards. Both debates include heated arguments that jobs are being siphoned off from OECD countries to developing countries, and that governments are being drawn into a "race to the bottom" as they compete to attract corporate investors. Both debates have heated up in conjunction with "globalisation" and the parallel rise over the last two decades in the level of unemployment in Europe and of wage inequality and the number of working poor in the United States. These labour-market problems have in turn given rise to accusations of "social dumping".

The labour-standards debate, perhaps even more than the environmental-standards debate, has also been at the heart of controversy over regional integration agreements involving OECD countries — notably in conjunction with U.S. Congressional ratification of NAFTA and the European Community's Social Charter. The latter was envisaged precisely as a bulwark against competitive deregulation among EC (now European Union) governments that could lead them to lower labour standards in conjunction with the deregulatory programme required to complete the Single Market. NAFTA was ratified only after the addition of "side agreements" aimed at strengthening the enforcement of national labour standards and at protecting the environment (agreements whose effectiveness is nevertheless thought by many to be limited).

The labour-standards debate, more than the debate over environmental standards, has also become a sensitive issue in multilateral trade policy discussions. Some OECD governments actively take the position that a set of internationally recognisable "core" labour standards should be included in WTO discussions. (Core labour standards are defined as the right of workers to associate, i.e. to form independent unions of their choice, and to bargain collectively, including the right to strike; the prohibition of forced labour and of exploitative child labour; and non-discrimination in employment[21].)

These governments argue *i)* that core labour standards reflect basic human rights which should be observed in all countries, irrespective of a country's level of development; *ii)* that observance of these rights can stimulate economic development, and is thus in the interest of all workers (and countries) worldwide; and *iii)* that global observance of these rights would help to neutralise protectionist pressures, notably in high-wage countries, and thus strengthen political support for the open multilateral trading system. These governments further emphasise that multilateral discussions of core labour standards should not focus on specific rules on working conditions (e.g. minimum-wage levels), and would not be prejudicial to any country's pursuit of trade based on a comparative advantage in low-wage industries. Several major developing countries strongly oppose the proposal, however, on the grounds that it risks serving as a guise for trade protection directed especially against the labour-intensive products in which developing countries are most likely to be competitive.

The relevant question for our purposes is whether competition among governments to attract FDI is leading them to weaken their protection of workers' rights and their enforcement of labour standards. Are they lowering those standards, on a *de jure* or a *de facto* basis, thereby putting pressure on other governments to follow suit?

In answering this question, it is important to distinguish four inter-related phenomena, or issues, and the evidence that is relevant to each. One is the deterioration in real wages that has occurred in many developing countries, and the deterioration in the relative wages (and in some cases real wages) of low-skilled workers that has occurred in OECD countries, over the last two decades. A second is the movement by many governments around the world, in OECD and non-OECD countries, to deregulate their markets, including their labour markets, over the same period. A third is the trend in government policy on labour standards *per se* — including both "core" and other (e.g. minimum wage) labour standards. A fourth — to which we turn towards the end of our discussion — is the role of labour standards in FDI-location decisions. Each requires some comment.

First, the trend in wages: Numerous studies have documented the serious deterioration in the relative and in some cases the absolute average wage levels of lower-skilled workers in OECD countries since the 1970s[22] — a deterioration which goes far to explain the criticisms of "globalisation" and accusations of "social dumping" heard widely in some OECD countries. Most studies of the causes of this deterioration argue that the domestic skill-biased employment effects of technological change and the transition from rigid taylorist to flexible post-taylorist systems of organisation explain the deterioration, with there being some disagreement on the relative importance of trade *per se*[23]. Significant declines in wage rates have also occurred since the 1980s in some developing-country exporters of manufactures (even before the turmoil that started in Asia in 1997), notably in Latin America. Those declines have mostly come in the wake of the 1980s debt crisis, the collapse of import-substitution industrialisation, macroeconomic instability, and — most directly significant for workers' real wages and living standards — major currency devaluations. Growing wage inequality has also coincided with trade-policy liberalisation in a number of these countries, though the cause of the growing inequality in these countries seems, as in OECD countries, to be more the skill-biased effects of technological and organisational change which is stimulated by trade liberalisation, than freer trade *per se*[24].

A second, related, phenomenon is the global trend towards market deregulation and economic policy liberalisation. In non-OECD countries, major political change and a marked reorientation of economic and industrial policy away from *dirigisme* towards more market-friendly policy regimes — often coming in the wake of major economic difficulties — have led over the last two decades to a widespread process of market deregulation, regulatory reform and trade and investment policy liberalisation. The process began, slowly, in China in 1979; it has been implemented much more widely in Latin America since the mid-1980s; it began in India in 1991; it was progressing gradually in many other Asian developing countries before the current turmoil (and may now accelerate in some and be delayed in others); and it was launched in Central and Eastern Europe with the collapse of communism in those countries. In OECD countries, the move over the last two decades to deregulate markets and liberalise trade and investment policies was initially stimulated by the stagnation of productivity growth followed by the emergence of *stagflation* in the late 1970s, and given some renewed impetus, notably in Europe — particularly as regards labour-market deregulation in continental Europe — by prolonged high unemployment in continental Europe.

One cannot, therefore, attribute significant responsibility for the worldwide movement towards deregulation, regulatory reform and more market-friendly policy regimes to increased global competition among governments to attract FDI *per se*. Insofar as there is a causal relationship between the global trends over the last two decades towards market deregulation and economic policy liberalisation, on the one hand, and towards intensifying competition for FDI, on the other, the relationship actually seems more to work in the opposite direction, with liberalisation of trade and investment policies and market deregulation (and a growing worldwide similarity in economic policy regimes as a result) tending to stimulate competition among governments to attract FDI. All one can say, in sum, is that competition to attract FDI is probably stimulated by, and may in turn help to reinforce, the policy trend towards economic policy liberalisation and market deregulation — i.e. the two phenomena (liberalisation cum market deregulation and competition for FDI) may well be mutually reinforcing.

A third phenomenon is the trend in government policies on labour standards (it is an issue, and will remain so, if only because evidence on the trend is weak). What evidence there is of *de jure* or *de facto* change in government policies on labour standards — whether or not the change is to attract FDI — does not lend much support to the view that there is a "race to the bottom" in governments' defence of labour standards in the sense of an actual decline in those standards. What the evidence cannot show, of course, is whether *in the absence* of competition for FDI, governments' policies on labour standards would have been significantly different from what they are.

Data gathered by the OECD on freedom-of-association rights in 75 countries since about 1980 — countries which together account for virtually all world trade and all inward and outward FDI[25] — shed some useful light on this issue. These data reveal very significant differences in labour standards among countries, with at least some restrictions imposed on workers' freedom of association in *most* non-OECD countries, and no significant restrictions imposed on that freedom in OECD countries other than Mexico and Turkey (and Korea, which joined the OECD after the data were gathered)[26]. This fact alone could lead many people to subscribe to the view that many low-wage countries engage in "social dumping".

Equally important for our purpose — which is to try to identify the relationship between labour standards and competition for FDI — however, is the fact that the data show no significant *deterioration* in freedom-of-association rights in any of the 75 countries since the early 1980s, i.e. during the period for which the data were gathered — a period that coincides well with the period during which competition for FDI has heated up. The data also show significant improvement in those rights in 17 countries (Argentina, Brazil, nine other countries in Latin America, Korea, Chinese Taipei, the Philippines, Thailand, Turkey and Fiji). This improvement has come with the move to democracy in many of those countries.

Export-processing Zones

Also important to this issue is the evidence on the phenomenal growth of export-processing zones (EPZs) in developing countries since the 1970s. (Variously called free trade zones or industrial free zones, special economic zones, *maquiladores*, bonded warehouses, science and technology parks and free ports as well, the distinguishing feature of EPZs is their establishment by governments with the aim of attracting investment in export-oriented manufacturing or assembly plants by providing customs treatment to equipment and materials for assembly that enter the zones which is better [usually duty free] than the treatment they give to goods entering the rest of the economy; governments frequently provide infrastructure and other fiscal incentives to investors in the zones as well.) Today, according to ILO figures, about 27 million people (including 18 million in China), a high proportion of them young women, work in some 850 EPZs around the world (124 in China); and an increasing number of governments are considering establishing EPZs[27].

Many people see the proliferation of EPZs as a clear sign of intensifying policy competition to attract FDI; more than a few think it is evidence of a "race to the bottom" in labour standards. Adequate labour standards and a sound system of labour-management relations are, indeed, widely lacking in EPZs, as noted in a recent ILO study[28]. The study also notes that in three countries, namely Bangladesh, Pakistan and Zimbabwe, trade unions are even forbidden in EPZs — in Bangladesh and Pakistan since the early 1980s, in Zimbabwe since the EPZ was created in 1994.

The ILO study nevertheless also reports that "the vast majority of EPZs are covered by the national labour laws of their country, and ... physical conditions of work inside the zones are frequently better than those outside the zone"[29]. It observes that national minimum labour standards and industrial-relations legislation apply in most zones, as do minimum-wage rates. It further observes that those minimum-wage rates are commonly higher than outside the zones (Bangladesh is a case in point), and workers' take-home pay is often higher in the zones than in comparable factories outside the EPZ.

Looking to the future, the ILO study also points up the growing pressures on EPZ-operating countries to adapt to what it refers to as the "new logic of global production" and to the transition in the OECD economies, and in global investors' production systems, from taylorist to more flexible post-taylorist types of organisation[30]. The study usefully distinguishes three broad types of response by firms in EPZs to increasing global competition:

— *Intensification*. Some firms try to compete by "sweating" labour, making workers work harder and longer, until they burn out and leave. Shifts get longer and longer, the workplace trends to be oppressive (guards often patrol the plant floor, and all entrances and exits, including fire-escapes, are commonly locked), there is little consultation between workers and mangers, production is inefficient and error-prone with high wastage rates, high labour turnover, tardiness and absenteeism. Intensification thus reaches a limit beyond which it becomes counter-productive, plagued by falling productivity, deteriorating quality and growing labour unrest.

— *Motivation*. Some managers seek to motivate workers by introducing cash incentives for higher productivity, regular attendance and long service, offer free transportation to and from work and free breakfast to workers (thereby helping to ensure they arrive on time, reduce the fatigue of having to walk long distances and are strong enough to work a solid shift), often provide medical and dental services (to improve workers' health), crèche facilities, air conditioning to improve productivity, housing services to workers who come from other regions and, in some cases set up consumer co-operatives and savings co-operatives for workers. These incentives nevertheless reach a plateau, and the need continuously to improve on speed, quality and cost oblige management to look further for productivity gains.

— *Participation*. A growing number of managers seek to involve workers in meeting the challenge of speed-quality-cost improvements by introducing teams, their gradual empowerment, increased sharing of information, joint problem-solving and target-setting, and the encouragement of worker innovation. The most successful firms have developed a sense of partnership between labour and management, given workers a real sense of ownership of the outcomes, cultivated the leadership and decision-making qualities of team workers, and begun to see the role of management as one of supporting and co-ordinating worker initiative — with considerable attitudinal change required from both managers and workers. Supervisors are being eliminated as teams are becoming more self-directed and "empowered", technicians are being trained to replace the assistant engineers who are being sent to university to become full engineers, and the professional engineers move into management or R&D; multi-skilling of workers, achieved with training actively encouraged by managers, is reducing the number of skill layers, increasing the value added by each layer and deepening job satisfaction, and the entire enterprise moves to a flatter structure with more value added by each individual. Workers appreciate the possibilities for personal advancement, greater earning capacity and expanded responsibility, and a dynamic process of productivity growth is in motion[31].

The ILO study leaves little doubt about the direction of change being imposed on firms in EPZs by market forces: "Today, globalisation places the emphasis on speed, efficiency and quality as well as cost ... shifting the focus from cheap labour to productive labour. This realisation is changing the way governments, employers, and even trade union organisations view human resource issues. For countries to remain competitive, they must get this mix of cost and quality factors right by raising the capacity of their human resources, ensuring stable labour relations, and improving the working and living conditions of zone workers"[32]. Squarely addressing policy makers, the study further notes that in the absence of such a transformation, and of EPZ incentives that relate to a clear set of development objectives, "what is meant to be a set of incentives to attract investors can be a *disincentive* to retaining them and to local development"[33].

With all the labour problems, and low labour standards, that exist in EPZs, and the marked proliferation of EPZs in recent years, one cannot doubt the need for strengthening governments' individual and collective efforts to ensure global enforcement of core labour rights[34]. Workers' right to freedom of association is still very far from being universally recognised and enforced as it should be. It is equally true, however, that, with the exception of Zimbabwe, one cannot point to empirical evidence of a downward trend in government enforcement of labour standards *per se*. Though gradual, the trend in labour standards *per se* actually seems to be one of improvement and, if the ILO study on EPZs is correct, the transition to post-taylorist flexible production systems by OECD-based investors means that market forces should work to increase that rate of improvement in developing countries.

One can still hypothesise, of course, that competition among governments to attract FDI has restrained that rate of improvement over the last two decades. Available evidence does not allow us meaningfully to address the counter-factual question of what would have happened in the absence of such competition. This hypothesis does however lead us to the fourth issue cited at the beginning of this section, namely the role of labour standards in investors' location decisions.

Here again, insufficient evidence makes any conclusion tentative. The OECD labour standards study approaches it by looking at the relationship between countries' level of enforcement of core labour standards (mainly freedom of association and collective-bargaining rights) and their trade competitiveness. The study finds little correlation: "empirical findings confirm ... that core labour standards do not play a significant role in shaping trade performance"[35]. In other words, there is no empirical support for the view that low-standards countries will enjoy gains in export-market shares — and thus in their attractiveness to export-oriented FDI — to the detriment of high-standards countries. For policy makers in low-wage countries, the clear implication is that they have little to gain, in terms of their ability to attract FDI, by failing to observe and enforce core labour standards.

The OECD study also notes that there is no evidence that low core labour standards are even associated with low unit labour costs: real wages actually grew faster than productivity growth in a fair number of low-standards countries from the mid-1980s to the mid-1990s. The study concludes that investors are likely to prefer a stable social climate (which is likely to be associated with "good" standards and consistent enforcement) over one characterised by low standards and social tension[36]. All of this implies that when wage levels and labour costs are driven upward by market forces, governments are ill-advised to try to keep them down artificially, in attempting to attract FDI, by failing to protect workers' rights and enforce labour standards. It also suggests that FDI-location decisions are not significantly affected by labour standards *per se* — or, more accurately, that low labour standards are not an attraction and can be a deterrent to most FDI.

The ILO study on EPZs reaches a similar conclusion. It observes that, "Countries which have established trade union presence in the zones do not appear to have suffered any loss of investment" and that, "None of the enterprises interviewed [for the ILO study] stated that a lack of worker organisation was an incentive to invest"[37].

Evidence that governments have little to gain by lowering labour standards is also provided by A. Raynauld and J.P. Vidal in a study that looks at the relationship between labour standards as a whole (not just core standards) and competitiveness. It shows empirically that since 1980, countries with low labour standards have not attracted a greater share of global FDI, and those with high standards have maintained or increased their share of global FDI inflows; countries with low standards have not increased their share of global exports; and two-thirds of 39 countries with low labour standards have seen their international competitiveness, as measured by unit labour costs, stagnate or decline (a decline reflects either a decline in labour productivity relative to the nominal cost of labour or a rise in the nominal cost of labour relative to its productivity) while 14 of 18 high-standards countries have increased their international competitiveness[38].

Labour Market Deregulation

Our discussion of the effects of competition for FDI on labour standards would not be complete without two further comments on the origin of the pressure in recent years to deregulate labour markets in OECD countries, notably in Europe. First, as Bachtler *et al.* note, while the debate in Europe over "social dumping" was initially regarded as an investment issue between developed and developing countries, it has emerged as largely an investment and policy-competition issue among governments *within* Europe. The United Kingdom's refusal in 1991 to sign the EC Social Charter was a major cause of this emergence, as was the 1993 Hoover Company's decision to relocate a plant from France to Scotland to take advantage of workforce concessions (on working arrangements, a no-strike agreement and exclusion of new employees from pension rights for two years) which the French workers would have been forbidden to make under French law. Second, labour-market deregulation — especially since the recession of the early 1990s, which marked the beginning of intense pressures in many continental European countries to deregulate their labour markets — has largely been motivated by governments' desire to enhance labour-market flexibility in their economies so as to reduce disincentives to *existing* firms' expansion of investment and employment, rather than as a means to compete for FDI. (Of course, this motivation has not prevented the UK government, in particular, from seeking to draw attention to its relatively high degree of deregulation as a means to enhance the UK's attractiveness to foreign investors[39].)

As European integration proceeds — as the Single Market becomes an economic and monetary reality — and firms across Europe continue to restructure and integrate on a regional basis, investors' location decisions can be expected to become more sensitive to regulatory differences among governments, particularly as those differences relate to firms' desire for flexibility. This suggests that the scope for regulatory competition in Europe may increase. However, there has also been significant convergence of EU labour-market policies, as governments in continental Europe move (sometimes with difficulty) to more flexible policies, on the one hand, and the new UK Labour Government agreed to sign the Social Charter, on the other. This convergence suggests *less* scope for regulatory competition in the future, and that the impact of deregulation on FDI-location decisions may diminish. The result of these contradictory forces, as Bachtler *et al.* observe, may be to shift policy competition towards policy areas that remain outside the purview of the European Commission, notably including social-security tax competition[40].

The direction of change in Europe, if unchecked, may thus be similar to that observed in the United States, where competition among state governments to attract corporate investment and the free-rider problem have long made it difficult to devise a satisfactory approach to unemployment insurance. Such competition — much more than international competition with developing countries — also reportedly contributes to the low US rate of private-sector unionisation (by OECD standards) and to the downward pressure in the United States on such labour standards as minimum safety conditions and "workers' compensation" (insurance for workers injured on the job) since the 1970s[41].

The point to be emphasised for our purposes, however, is that governments in OECD countries — at the sub-national or national level — compete for FDI primarily with *one another*, and do so largely within their own geographical region. The negative effects of that competition — notably including some governments' overblown *fear* of losing FDI to low-wage countries — cannot be attributed, to any significant degree, to "social dumping" by low-wage countries, or to any "race to the bottom" in global labour standards caused by developing countries.

This does not mean, of course, that it would not be preferable for all countries to enforce core labour standards. Nor does it mean that competition among governments to attract FDI may not act as a deterrent to a socially optimal *raising* of labour standards (although the analogy with environmental standards is hazardous[42]). What it means is that policy makers in OECD countries must overcome their fear of losing FDI to low-wage countries, and must, in any case, use means other than weakening their protection of workers' rights and their enforcement of labour standards to seek to attract FDI. Policy makers in developing and emerging economies must also use rules-based means to attract FDI *other* than those that involve any downgrading of local labour standards; and they have no reason not to respect and enforce core labour standards.

More Effective Rules-based Policies to Attract FDI

While government policies on labour and environmental standards have been the subject of heated debate, other rules-based policies have been more effective as means to attract FDI.

Regional Integration Agreements

One of the most effective means has been regionalisation, i.e. regional integration agreements between two or more national governments. These agreements, which have proliferated since the mid-1980s in conjunction with the current wave of globalisation, have generated considerable controversy in their own right. Much of that controversy has focused on the question of the agreements' eventual "trade diversion" effects and their implications for the multilateral trading system[43]. Less widely discussed is the fact that the motivation driving many of these agreements, certainly in developing countries, is the desire to attract FDI.

NAFTA is an important case in point. Following the 1988 signing of the Canada-US Free Trade Agreement (whose implications for promoting bilateral FDI were of greater interest to both countries than its implications for promoting bilateral trade *per se*) Mexico sought to launch the NAFTA negotiations, in 1990, precisely as a means to increase the flow of FDI to Mexico[44]. Both the "announcement" effect and the actual agreement have, in fact, contributed substantially to Mexico's increased FDI inflows, from North America and from elsewhere, since then[45].

Another case in point is Mercosur. While the objectives of the agreement are multiple — political as well as economic — there can be no doubt that it has been a major attraction to FDI. Particularly revealing in this regard are the results of interviews reported in the Argentinean study undertaken for this project (cf. Chapter 2) which show that while the country's auto regime and the success of its macroeconomic stabilisation policy have been important to attracting FDI, even more important to the auto-company executives interviewed, in terms of its ability to attract FDI in their sector to Argentina, has been Mercosur.

Europe's experience is another important case in point, both as regards the years following the creation of the Common Market in 1957, with the signing of the Treaty of Rome, and with regard to the years following the decision, in 1985, to create the Single Market. Although the driving motivation behind European integration as a whole, and certainly behind the Treaty of Rome, has been more political than economic *per se* (to ensure against war in Europe), the effect in both periods has been to stimulate a major growth of FDI inflows, both from outside Europe and from within.

While the issue of trade "diversion" that might stem from regional integration agreements does not directly concern this study, it is also worth noting that free investment flows and the attraction that such agreements can exert on FDI inflows are likely to more than compensate for the small negative effects that might result from any trade diversion associated with today's (relatively open) regional integration agreements. More serious a problem may precisely be the *investment* diversion that these regional integration agreements can induce, as NAFTA has shown in the case of export-oriented FDI in the clothing sector that has been diverted to Mexico from many Caribbean countries whose economies depended heavily on that investment[46]. Singapore's decision to sign a bilateral "framework" agreement with the United States in 1992, and the decision by ASEAN countries to sign their own free trade agreement (AFTA) that same year, were reportedly motivated more by concern over NAFTA's possible diversion of investment away from ASEAN countries, than by concern over any static trade-diversion effects that NAFTA might cause. (It is in this same light that one must also apparently understand ASEAN countries' desires and fears today about creating an ASEAN Investment Area [AIA] — fears that reflect the perception in some ASEAN countries, since the emergence of the "Asian crisis" and the perceived danger of contagion effects, that in the current context it may be better to *differentiate* oneself from one's neighbours, than to integrate with them, in order to attract FDI.)

Clearly, however, and notwithstanding current doubts among ASEAN countries about plans to proceed with the creation of an AIA, regional integration agreements can be a powerful policy tool to attract FDI. This is true, above all, because of the power of attraction of the larger markets they create. Often, today, it is also true because of the extent to which regional integration agreements are associated with, or even used by governments as the principal vehicle to achieve, a greater degree of internal market deregulation[47].

At the same time, as noted earlier with regard to labour markets, such agreements can be used by governments to help ensure that a necessary process of deregulation or regulatory reform does not degenerate into an unmanaged and destructive process of *competitive* deregulation. They can be a good vehicle to facilitate co-operation among governments on the establishment and/or enforcement of labour, environmental, or other standards and regulations — and can help governments collectively to defend socially optimal standards and regulations that may be difficult for some governments to defend individually when faced with the pressures and prisoner's-dilemma nature of policy competition. They can also be a good vehicle to harmonise and regulate governments' use of fiscal and financial incentives to attract FDI, and to overcome the prisoner's-dilemma nature of incentives-based competition.

Privatisation and the Need for Competition Policy

Closely associated with the processes of domestic market deregulation and the liberalisation of international trade and investment policy in many countries, both OECD and non-OECD, has been the privatisation of state-owned enterprises. During the 1980s and 1990s, privatisation is estimated to have generated over $500 billion in revenues, including a bit less than $400 billion in OECD countries and over $100 billion in developing and emerging economies. As of end-1998, Latin American countries accounted for slightly under two-thirds of the latter figure, and Asian countries for about 30 per cent.

A large proportion of the revenues generated by privatisation in developing and emerging economies has come through FDI, making privatisation a significant source of attraction to FDI, notably in Latin America during the 1990s. Here is not the place to enter into a discussion of the advantages and disadvantages of privatisation *per se*, or of different approaches to privatisation. What is important to stress, is that a policy to attract FDI should not rely too exclusively on privatisation (if only because of the limits imposed on such policy by the value of privatiseable assets) and that the long-term benefits of such a policy may depend heavily on the extent to which a country's move to privatise state-owned assets is accompanied by an effective policy to ensure vigorous and sustained price competition on the domestic market.

This observation about the importance of competition policy is particularly important for developing and emerging economies, where such a policy is often lacking, and where concentrated monopolistic and oligopolistic structures of local economic and political power often create rigidities that constitute a major hindrance to development. Transforming a public monopoly into a private one, by offering investors a protected market for example, is a common temptation because it increases the market value of assets to be privatised. It is a temptation that must be resisted. The broader point for policy makers, especially in developing and emerging economies where FDI accounts for a large proportion of privatised assets, is the importance of developing a sound competition policy — perhaps including the establishment of an independent and pro-active competition agency — to operate in tandem with policies, including privatisation, to attract FDI[48].

Accountability and Rules-based Governance

No discussion of rules-based competition among governments to attract FDI, especially among governments in developing and emerging economies, would be complete without mention of the tremendous importance some investors — especially those seeking sites for long-term investment in major production capabilities to serve regional and global markets, i.e. those which governments are generally most eager to attract — attach to the *stability* and *predictability* of the operating environment of their chosen investment sites. This observation brings us back, of course, to the importance of the fundamentals, notably political and macroeconomic stability, along with market size and growth potential, and the availability of infrastructure and human resources. The point, however, is that countries that do reasonably well on the fundamentals are now finding that strengthening their *judiciary system*, or having a judiciary system that is seen both at home and abroad as fair and consistent, and as having the power and independence to enforce its decisions, can be a powerful attraction — or its absence a significant deterrent — to many investors.

Among the more sensitive investors in this regard are those whose investable assets include advanced technologies or valuable intellectual property in manufacturing and in modern services, i.e. precisely the kind of assets that many governments are most desirous to attract. For some of these investors, the recognition and enforcement of *intellectual property rights* are of critical importance.

Beyond the matter of the judiciary system, finally, is the broader issue of the government's credibility — first of all as regards macroeconomic policy, but ultimately as regards policy as a whole. Integral to this issue are the degree of *transparency* of policy choices and the *accountability* of policy makers. While a system based on negotiated incentives to attract investors may appeal to many investors, as well as to some government officials, most investors profit more, in the long run, from the stability, transparency and predictability of a rules-based approach to FDI policy.

Some countries, such as Singapore, may find it feasible and profitable to pursue both a strong rules-based approach *and* an active incentives-based approach to attracting FDI. The strength of Singapore's success in incentives-based competition nevertheless owes a lot to the strength of its rules-based approach. So, indeed, does Singapore's apparent ability to avoid the damaging excesses of rent-seeking behaviour and corruption that can easily be associated with the active use of discretionary investment incentives, especially by national governments, in the absence of a strong and stable national rules-based approach to FDI policy.

Whether Singapore constitutes a model for other countries to emulate is, in important respects, a moot question. The lesson it seems to offer is the importance for national governments to establish, and maintain, a solid track record of stability, credibility and internal accountability — a *sound rules-based approach* to promoting and attracting real investment in the economy — whether or not the government chooses to offer fiscal and financial incentives to attract specific corporate investors.

Notes

1.   Castleman (1979). The 1970s did in fact witness a major wave of relocation of manufacturing capacities to low-wage "export platform" production sites in some developing countries. It was largely a response to the combined effects of the marked slowdown of productivity growth at home and the growing penetration of the US market, for the first time, by many Japanese and European manufacturers. The pressures on US firms to cut costs and gain flexibility did indeed intensify considerably during the 1970s. (Cf. Oman, 1994, 1996a).

2.   Tobey (1990).

3.   Petroleum and gas, chemicals and related products, and primary and fabricated metals are the main "environmentally sensitive" industries in which FDI is important.

4.   According to Repetto, for example, 1992 data show 84 per cent of US FDI in pollution-intensive industries going to other OECD countries, as compared to 49 per cent in other industries, and only 5 per cent of the FDI going to developing countries in pollution-intensive industries. He also notes that the stock of FDI in the pollution-intensive industries represents a smaller share of total FDI stock in most developing countries than in the 1960s and 1970s (cf. Repetto, 1995).

5.   See, for example, Esty and Mendelsohn (1995).

6.   *Ibid.*

7.   World Wide Fund for Nature (1998).

8.   See, for example, Schmidheiney and Gentry (1997).

9.   UNCTAD (1993).

10.   See Oman (1994) and Blömstrom and Kokko (1996).

11.   While our interest in this study is to understand the effects of *competition to attract* FDI, rather than to analyse the effects of FDI *per se*, it is worth noting that FDI can also promote the diffusion of environmentally friendly technologies through the expansion of the environmental goods and services industry, and that worldwide sales of pollution abatement equipment and related services reached $200 billion by the mid-1990s, with predictions of fast growth in the coming years (cf. OECD, 1997b; and Duchin *et al.*, 1995).

12.   Bachtler *et al.*, p. 111.

13.   *Ibid.*

14. OECD (1997*a*).

15. Reported in Gentry and Fernandez (1976).

16. Christie and Rolfe with Legard (1995).

17. See Birdsall and Wheeler (1992). The quotation is from Lucas, Wheeler and Hettige (1992).

18. Bachtler *et al.*, p. 112.

19. *Ibid.*, p. 139 (emphasis in the original).

20. One hindrance to such co-ordination is of course that when the ecological benefits are transboundary, national governments are more apt to neglect them since many of those who reap them are outside the country. However, as one of the most fervent advocates of international environmental policy co-ordination points out, the main stumbling block may be the "seemingly entrenched gap between rich and poor nations. The fact that much environmental damage is a consequence of consumption demands in the developed countries means that, according to the 'polluter pays' principle, they should bear most of the clean-up costs. ... Developing countries, at least initially, must be allowed greater flexibility in implementing environmental standards, as embedded in Principle 17 of the Rio Accords, on common but differentiated responsibilities. This [stumbling block] is exemplified by the Kyoto Protocol which will not be ratified by the US Senate until an — unspecified — level of 'meaningful participation' of developing countries is achieved" (World Wide Fund for Nature, 1998, p. 7).

21. See OECD (1996).

22. See Lawrence (1996) and OECD (1994).

23. See Lawrence (1996), Wood (1994) and Rodrik (1996 and 1997). On the impact of the transition from taylorist to post-taylorist systems of work organisation, see Oman (1996*a*).

24. Robbins (1996).

25. OECD (1996).

26. For example, strikes are prohibited in China, "practically prohibited" in Egypt, Iran and Syria, and "very difficult" in Pakistan and Tanzania. Collective bargaining is seriously restricted in Malaysia (in Pioneer Industries), in Singapore (in new enterprises) and in China and Thailand (in state enterprises). Countries where "some restrictions [on freedom of association] exist, but it is possible to establish independent workers' organisations and union confederations" include Argentina, Brazil, Chile, Ecuador, Jamaica, Mexico, Peru, Venezuela, Hong Kong, India, Ethiopia, Niger, South Africa and Zambia. At one extreme are countries where "freedom of association is practically inexistent": China, Indonesia, Egypt, Iran, Kuwait, Syria and Tanzania. At the other extreme are countries where "freedom of association is by and large guaranteed in law and practice": OECD countries, other than Mexico and Turkey, plus the Bahamas, Barbados, Surinam, Malta and Israel. Other countries fall into the category of those where "restrictions on freedom of association are significant ... the existence of stringent registration requirements, political interference or acts of anti-union discrimination make it very difficult to form independent workers' organisations or union confederations" (*ibid.*, pp. 42-43).

27. Mexico, with about 900 000 people employed in its *maquila* sector, is the second largest EPZ-operating country. Others include Malaysia, Sri Lanka, Mauritius, Bangladesh, Pakistan, Indonesia, the Philippines, about a dozen countries in Central America and the Caribbean, Colombia, Brazil, Kenya, Egypt, Zimbabwe, Jordan and Turkey. See ILO (1998*a*).

28. *Ibid.*, pp. 21-28. See also Nowicki (1998).

29. ILO (1998*a*).

30. See also Oman (1994 and 1996*b*).

31. ILO (1998*a*), pp. 41-44. The study further notes, "The most advanced use of this approach is in the highly capital intensive electronics plants which need to amortise their investments quickly by operating non-stop at very high rates of productivity. ... In the Philippines the [ILO's] Action Programme found companies sending workers on the sort of outward bound survival courses normally reserved for top management in order to enhance their decision-making capacity" (p. 43).

32. *Ibid.*, pp. 39-40. Citing examples of significant reform of labour and investment law in more than a half-dozen EPZ-operating countries since 1996, the study concludes, "Zones which can offer high quality human resources, training facilities and labour-relations services such as conciliation and mediation are more likely to attract and retain investors of world standard" (p. 41). Elsewhere it observes, "The labour laws of many developing countries are a legacy of the colonial era. They are often cumbersome and heavy on administration. ... The most effective legislative reforms provide for systems which are less administration-intensive, simple, easy-to-use, and can be quickly adapted to take account of changing circumstances. Many zones have their own system of labour administration, often staffed by ex-officials of the Ministry of Labour, but now paid for by the zone, and with responsibility for monitoring minimum standards, resolving conflicts, and providing labour-relations advisory services to employers and workers" (p. 40).

33. *Ibid.*, p. 14.

34. For a discussion of the crucial issue of mechanisms to promote core labour standards worldwide, see OECD (1996).

35. *Ibid.*, p. 105.

36. Thus, as the OECD labour-standards study further notes, "any fear on the part of developing countries that better core standards would negatively affect their economic performance or competitive position ... has no economic rationale. On the contrary, it is conceivable that the observance of core standards would strengthen the long-term economic performance of all countries"(*ibid.*).

37. ILO (1998*a*), p. 12.

38. Raynauld and Vidal (1998).

39. The OECD study on *Trade, Employment and Labour Standards* also notes that ILO experts raised the question of whether protection against dismissal of strikers was adequate in the United Kingdom, a question which the 1994 Conference Committee answered by noting that UK protection against anti-union discrimination had strengthened (OECD, 1996, p. 42).

40. Bachtler *et al.*, *op. cit.*, p. 132.

41. Donahue, pp. 5-6.

42. Any comparison between the effects of competition for FDI on government policies on the environment and the effects of such competition on their labour-standards policies is less than straightforward because the "market failures" associated with environmental "spillovers" are very different from those that require governments to protect workers' rights and enforce labour standards.

43. The literature on the welfare effects of regional integration agreements traditionally distinguishes between "static" and "dynamic" effects. Static effects refer to the impact on allocative efficiency with member countries' productive capacity taken as given (i.e. static) whereas dynamic effects refer to the impact on that capacity (thus including the effects of such agreements on investment flows, which the static effects exclude). Traditional customs union theory, as developed by Jacob Viner in 1950, distinguishes between two types of static effect: "trade creation" and "trade diversion". The former refers to the fact that, for any country participating in a customs union (or similar regional integration agreement), participation in the union reduces the price of imports from other countries in the union (because of the elimination of tariffs between them), thereby creating trade between them (at the expense of less efficient domestic suppliers in each country) and thus enhancing the members' collective welfare. Simultaneously, however, the union causes "trade diversion" in the sense that as countries joining the union move from a situation where each country's import protection is directed against all other countries to a situation where there is protection against non-members but no longer against other members of the union, the move drives a wedge between the price of imports from members and those from non-members, thereby diverting trade from the latter to the former, and thus, generally, reducing *members'* collective welfare. (Trade creation is also normally good, and trade diversion bad, for non-members' welfare, insofar as they trade with members of the customs union.)

    What ultimately counts, of course, is the net result of the two effects (trade creation and trade diversion) combined, about which no general prediction can be made. That result is an empirical matter which depends on the particular configuration and workings of each regional integration agreement. All one can say is that certain factors are likely to favour trade creation over trade diversion, namely the existence of a high proportion of intra-regional trade (as a share of members' total trade) before the agreement was made; a large number of members; low transportation costs among members; and low protection vis-à-vis non-members.

    As to the dynamic effects, it is widely agreed that regional integration can have substantial positive growth effects on members through the higher productivity that can result from greater competition and better exploitation of economies of scale. Of course, stronger growth is "trade creating" for non-members insofar as members' income-elasticity of demand for imports is above zero.

    For further discussion, see Oman (1994 and 1996a).

44. See Peres (1990).

45. Mexico's average FDI inflow rose from about $2.6 billion in 1985-90 to $4.5 billion in 1991-93 and $8.5 billion in 1994-96 (despite, in this last period, the effect of the country's financial crisis).

46. ILO (1998*a*), p. 16, reports that 150 firms and 123 000 jobs have been lost in the clothing industry in the Caribbean since the introduction of NAFTA, many of them having relocated to Mexico (whose clothing exports to the United States rose from $709 million in 1990 to $3.8 billion in 1996). See also note 2 in Chapter 4 on the March 1999, US initiative to give "NAFTA parity" to the Caribbean countries; and Mortimore and Peres (1998).

47. See Oman (1994 and 1996*a*) for a fuller discussion of why regional integration agreements can usefully serve as policy means to achieve desired internal deregulation in the face of resistance from internally entrenched oligopolistic interest groups.

48. See Oman (1996) .

Chapter 4

Conclusions

Clearly, competition among governments to attract corporate investment is widespread and can be intense. It involves state or provincial governments in both OECD and non-OECD countries, and to a lesser but growing degree municipal governments, as much as it involves national governments. It affects policy making in those governments, as well as investment-location decisions, and as barriers to international investment diminish, the significance of the competition increases.

One key international policy question is whether the prisoner's-dilemma nature of this competition calls for collective action by governments, including OECD governments, either to limit the competition, or to limit its negative effects. Another key policy question concerns the effect of policy competition on today's developing and emerging economies, and its implications for policy makers in those countries. The evidence provides no simple answer to either question.

Is the Competition Intensifying?

One reason the evidence provides no simple answer is that it does not clearly point up a likely intensification of the competition in the future. While the competition is intense today, there is no particular reason why it should become *more* intense in the coming years — and there are a few reasons why it may not.

One reason why the competition may not further intensify is that the remarkable upsurge in global FDI flows that has occurred since the mid-1980s (in relation to global trade flows, and as a share of global output) has clearly been a *stimulus* to, not the consequence of, governments' giving greater attention to attracting FDI inflows (as governments have been stimulated not to miss out on attracting "their share" of that investment growth). While the relatively high current level of global FDI flows may or may not continue in the longer run, there is little reason to expect a *further* surge in its level relative to those of world trade and output.

113

A second reason why policy competition for FDI probably will not further intensify is that while numerous countries have turned away from relatively *dirigiste* inward-oriented development strategies over the last 15 years — strategies that were often seen by foreign corporations as relatively hostile to FDI — most countries have now made that shift in policy orientation. Again, the competition may remain intense, but there is little cause to believe it will become *more* intense.

A third reason is the apparent extent to which incentives-competition, in particular, and the high value of incentives sometimes reported in the press, tends to be concentrated in one particular industry: the auto industry. That industry has witnessed major investments in new production capacities over the 1980s and 1990s in both OECD and non-OECD countries as it has gone through a global process of restructuring and shifted from taylorist mass-production to post-taylorist "lean" or flexible production methods in the advanced economies; but the coming years are unlikely to see comparable levels of investment in the creation of additional new capacities worldwide, even as the process of restructuring continues.

None of this means, of course, that incentives competition will diminish, even in such countries as Brazil or the United States where much of the very visible incentives-competition among state governments has been for investment projects in this one sector. It simply means that one cannot point to any significant likelihood of a *further intensification* of that competition in the coming years.

The limited data that are available on actual *trends* in the supply of investment incentives also tend, on balance, to support the view that there is no secular trend towards an intensification of competition that is likely to continue into the future. The best data are those of the countries of the European Union, and they clearly support this view — whether the reason is the ability of the European Commission to regulate "State aids" or the budgetary constraints faced by individual EU countries. But even in such countries as Singapore and Malaysia, which have long been major users of fiscal incentives to attract FDI, there is no evidence of any significant *intensification* of that use in the recent period. Only in the United States, among the countries covered in this study, do estimates of the approximate cost of incentives to the governments that supply them point to a clear escalation of that cost over a significant period of time (consistent with the hypothesis of a prolonged incentives "bidding war"), and those estimates all refer to the auto sector.

The Effects of Policy Competition

While worldwide policy competition to attract corporate investment may not be intensifying, it certainly is, and probably will remain, intense and widespread — "pervasive" as the UNCTAD report put it. The question of the effects of that competition is thus critical.

In addressing this question, one can usefully distinguish three broad categories of effects: *i)* those on investment *per se*, both as regards investors' location decisions and as regards the aggregate supply of investment; *ii)* those on government behaviour and policy making; *iii)* those on the economy.

Effects on Investment Decisions

Only in recent years have academic studies begun to recognise the ability of incentives and other discretionary government actions aimed at attracting FDI to be very effective. For years, the overwhelming importance of the economic and political fundamentals in investment decisions was interpreted by most academics to mean that discretionary taxing and spending decisions or other discretionary government actions to attract FDI were largely ineffective and therefore wasteful or, at best, useless; today, the weight of expert opinion is shifting to a position of greater uncertainty about the effectiveness of incentives.

The evidence in this study is clearly and broadly consistent with an interpretation of investment-location decisions as consisting of a two-stage (or multi-stage) process in which investors first establish a "short list" of potential sites that satisfy their requirements for the type of location they are seeking, including satisfactory "fundamentals". Once investors have established such a "short list" many will then, and only then, consider the availability — or even seek to generate offers — of incentives which the governments in whose jurisdictions those sites are located are willing to provide, or negotiate, before the final site selection is made. At this stage in the location decision-making process, incentives and other discretionary government offers can be decisive.

It can be counterproductive, on the other hand, for governments to offer significant incentives to attract investors if the economy or potential investment sites under their jurisdiction fail to meet the fundamentals criteria or other basic requirements of investors. Such offers not only tend to fail to attract the kinds of investment sought, they tend to "soften" the credibility of the governments that make them and thus further weaken their ability to attract solid investors. Thus, while skilfully targeting specific investors can have positive effects, as Singapore's experience shows, it is equally true that undiscerning policy competition can actually have a negative effect on FDI inflows — and it is probably this second lesson that too many governments fail to grasp.

The evidence also fails to support the hypothesis that more intense policy competition for FDI tends to increase the aggregate supply of FDI. In numerous countries there has been a simultaneous increase in policy competition and FDI inflows. However, the causal relationship almost certainly has worked in the opposite direction, i.e. the significant growth of FDI has spurred competition among governments that want to be sure to attract "their share" of that FDI while its growth lasts. There is little evidence, in particular, that the phenomenal growth in the global supply of FDI since the mid-1980s has been a response to increased incentives — or to less government protection of the environment or of workers' rights and labour standards. While "globalisation" may well have spurred the global growth of FDI, it has been much more a cause than a consequence of heightened policy competition for FDI over the last 15 years.

Effects on Policy Making

There is little empirical evidence to support the strong versions of the "race to the bottom" hypotheses concerning governments' defence of labour and environmental standards. The danger of such "races" — or at least of a building up of downward pressures on those standards — does however exist. Nor can the evidence tell us to what extent competition might be inhibiting a socially optimal *raising* of those standards. Vigilance and monitoring are therefore required to ensure that competition among governments to attract investment does not undermine those standards, or the level of their enforcement.

The evidence also shows, however, that the competition for FDI exerts some *upward* pressure on labour and environmental standards. This pressure arises as governments, particularly local governments, in developing and emerging economies as well as in OECD countries compete, increasingly, to attract investments in relatively "clean" and knowledge- or skills-intensive manufacturing and service industries. The pressure arises because investors in these industries increasingly seek out investment locations that offer relatively high environmental standards (sites where their managers and employees prefer to live, and that minimise pollution costs to their operations) and that ensure adequate long-term supplies of workers capable of responding to the much more demanding human-resource needs of flexible post-taylorist "lean" enterprises.

Also consistent with the "positive-sum game" hypothesis is the evidence on the effects of competition for FDI in inducing governments to increase or improve local supplies of infrastructure and human resources, be it through direct public investment or through regulatory and other policy reforms to induce more private investment in such "public" goods. Singapore is the outstanding example in support of this hypothesis, but there are others at both the national and sub-national level. There are, however, two important caveats. The evidence does not suggest that government moves to enhance local supplies of such productivity-enhancing public goods are primarily a response to the competition to attract FDI. Nor does it suggest that such moves are the primary means by which governments compete to attract FDI. Incentives, and/or rules-based means, such as regional integration, are the primary means, and it is unclear to what extent the financing of incentives comes at the expense of more investment in infrastructure and human resources. The evidence thus provides no more than weak support for the hypothesis that competition for FDI induces governments to enhance local supplies of productivity-enhancing public goods such as infrastructure and education.

Equally, if not more important, is the fact that in developing and emerging economies, in particular, policy competition for FDI is often associated with processes of political democratisation and of modernisation of the public sector. Brazil provides a good illustration. In that country, as in some others (e.g. China, India), policy competition for FDI among sub-national governments has been "activated" by, but also contributes to, a broader process of reform of policy making which includes regulatory reform, privatisation and liberalisation of trade and investment policies. This process strengthens market forces and induces sub-national governments to modernise and organise themselves better, and more flexibly, to enhance the competitiveness of the economies under their jurisdiction. Sub-national governments are learning not only how to negotiate incentives but to help investors identify investment opportunities, target potential investors, co-ordinate and professionalise their actions, and improve their own learning skills (and become "lean", more efficient and more responsive organisations themselves).

Many of the governments in developing and emerging economies — and the same can be said of OECD countries — that are most successful in competing to attract FDI thus tend precisely to be those that best meet the requirements for good government. These requirements notably include sound public finances — which in turn lend credibility to a government's concession of incentives in the eyes of investors, as well as legitimacy in the eyes of voters, because it is seen as unlikely to create an excessive and thus unsustainable fiscal or financial burden. Investors predominantly choose to invest in jurisdictions that present the lowest political and economic risk of suspending incentives. Equally important, investors seem often to choose sites where the government's strategy to attract investors is part of a broader process of mobilisation around a project of social and political reform in which the government redefines its role, turning away from the rigid structures and exclusive relationships with vested interest groups from the past ("traditional elites") in favour of greater democracy, transparency and competition. This process both enhances, and is reinforced by, the growing exposure of local and foreign firms in the domestic market to greater international competition.

The example of Brazil also serves to highlight the negative effects that policy competition for FDI can have on local policy making. The main "arena" for policy competition is the auto regime, which has strong discriminatory effects against auto parts producers in Brazil, and, even worse, creates a strong and unhealthy relationship of economic and political dependence between government and the auto industry. That relationship inevitably stimulates rent-seeking behaviour in the industry, including protectionist demands, which is amplified by policy competition and the excess production capacity that competition helps to generate. The result is also a *de facto* policy bias against small firms, and against exports.

The result could also be to fan conflict with neighbours — in this case Argentina — and to weaken the regional integration process (Mercosur). In fact, the result has been to induce Argentina to advance proposals for greater harmonisation of the countries' rules on sub-national governments' use of fiscal incentives and/or for the adoption of a single incentives regime for poorer regions throughout Mercosur. Policy competition for FDI may thus turn out to be a catalyst for the two countries to negotiate disciplines on investment incentives and other FDI-attraction policies within the context of Mercosur. The process is reminiscent of the steps Europe took, starting 40 years ago, in building its own Common Market.

Two final points regarding the effects of policy competition on policy making concern the "laboratory theory" and regional development policy. The first of these refers to the hypothesis that competition to attract investment will drive governments to experiment and thus generate valuable policy innovations, with the competitive process itself serving as a valuable test to weed out the less successful innovations. This hypothesis has notably been put forward by defenders of inter-state competition for investment in the United States. However, as the U.S. experience itself illustrates, the trend has rather been away from diversity and policy innovation, towards a growing similarity of policies and incentive packages with only the *cost* of those packages tending to rise in times of intense competition among governments.

The evidence on the effects of policy competition on policies whose declared objective is to favour the development of poorer areas or those suffering from high unemployment by stimulating investment in those areas is mixed. In OECD countries, the overall impact seems more to have been one of co-opting regional development policies for the pursuit of policy competition that does not mainly benefit the poorest segments of the population, or those most suffering from unemployment, than it does one of channelling the benefits of investment to those areas and segments of the population. In developing and emerging economies, one finds some evidence of policy competition benefiting poorer areas, as in the Northeast of Brazil. However, even in these countries, policy competition for FDI cannot be seen as a viable long-term substitute for explicit redistributional and regional development policies. The danger, in both OECD and non-OECD countries, is that the fiscal resources absorbed by policy competition will come precisely at the expense of more effective redistributional and regional development policies.

To reiterate, however, the greatest negative impact of policy competition on policy making is undoubtedly the "space" it creates for graft, corruption and rent-seeking behaviour (legal or illegal) as a whole — behaviour that can spread and infect policy making well beyond the realm of attracting FDI. This danger is particularly true of incentives-based competition, because of its virtually inherent lack of transparency. It points to the importance of channelling competition for FDI into *rules-based* forms of competition that do not weaken labour and environmental standards.

Economic Effects

Neither the investors who receive location incentives nor the government officials who supply them have proved willing to divulge sufficient information on the magnitude of those incentives to permit any meaningful aggregate cost-benefit analysis of policy competition. There are both "good" and "bad" reasons for this secrecy. They include governments' legitimate need for flexibility and to avoid setting precedents that have the effect of ratcheting-up incentive levels every time they increase their offer for one project, and investors' legitimate need to avoid revealing confidential business information to competitors, as well as the illegitimate reasons associated with graft, corruption and rent-seeking behaviour. The result is that the details of most incentive packages, or other discretionary government actions to attract particular investors, are never made public. The evidence that exists does, however, allow us to address several key issues.

One is the problem of market distortions. Incentives, in particular, can be seen as introducing distortions analogous to those caused by restrictions on trade. While the net cost of the static allocational inefficiencies caused by incentives for the global economy and for the countries that successfully use incentives to attract FDI are difficult to assess even on theoretical grounds — the extent to which corporate investors respond first to economic fundamentals, before allowing incentives to influence their location decisions, means this cost may not be too large — the cost to the "losers", i.e. the cost of incentives-induced investment *diversion* suffered by other potential host economies (other countries, or other locations within a country), can be significant. This cost is often reflected in significant (dynamic) trade diversion as well[1]. The many Caribbean Basin countries that have lost investment inflows and export shares in the clothing industry as a result of the investment (and export shares) which NAFTA has diverted to Mexico illustrate this danger[2].

Fear of such diversion, combined with governments' desire to attract "their share" of global corporate investment in a time of rapid globalisation and growth of global FDI (which, some governments also fear, may not last), is of course the main force driving policy competition. While fears that countries must compete for a globally fixed supply of corporate investment are unfounded — that supply will respond to changes in economic and political conditions in individual countries and worldwide — it is equally true that within specific sectors, or regions, governments' fears of investment diversion may be founded, and the cost of such diversion for losers can be significant.

Another type of distortion results from the tendency for policy competition, especially incentives, to favour large companies over small ones, thereby discriminating against the latter. While it is impossible to measure the cost of this distortion, that cost may be considerable. In most economies today, it is small and medium-size enterprises that provide the most dynamism as well as the most jobs and job growth. Policies to attract large firms must therefore be, and sometimes are, supported by other policies to compensate for discrimination against small firms — but when this happens, the result may in turn be to increase government involvement in the economy in ways, and at costs, that might be preferable to avoid.

A further type of distortion was mentioned previously: the co-optation by policy competition of regional development policy in many countries. Not only does this distortion entail the demonstrated cost of rendering regional development policies less efficient in terms of their declared objective, it increases the risk of rendering them counter-productive, i.e. of increasing regional disparities and income inequalities. The economic costs to the nominal beneficiaries of regional development policies (the poorer regions) can thus be significant — and so, therefore, can the social, political and ultimately the economic costs to the country as a whole.

A final distortion that deserves mention, but whose costs appear insignificant, is that of favouring foreign over domestic corporate investors. In fact, in most countries, government policies and actions to attract corporate investors make no formal or legal distinction between the two groups of investors — both are eligible to benefit from whatever incentives are offered or discretionary policies are undertaken to attract (or retain) corporate investment. However, in practice policy competition is often biased in favour of foreign investors, not because of their nationality (sometimes despite it), but because they tend to have more bargaining power than domestic investors. As newcomers they tend to be (and tend to be *seen* to be) more mobile or free in their choice of location; when entering a country they are more likely to create a significant number of jobs with one investment project; and their investment projects tend to be considerably larger than the average size of domestic firms' investment projects (which are usually for expansion). The cost of this distortion mainly takes the form of a bias against smaller firms, however, and does not seem to imply significant economic costs beyond those already discussed in that context.

Another major cost of policy competition, in addition to market distortions and the major indirect costs that can result from its negative effects on policy making, as is, of course, the direct cost to governments of the fiscal and financial incentives they give to investors. With estimates of that cost for individual investment projects sometimes amounting to hundreds of thousands of dollars *per job* that the project is directly to create — examples of such cost magnitudes are found in India and Brazil as well as in Canada, the United States and Europe, notably in the automobile industry — there can be no doubt of its significance.

A further question, however, is whether the direct cost of incentives is *too* high, in the sense of exceeding the benefits derived by the host economy from the investment project. To this question there is no simple answer. Part of the reason, of course, is the difficulty of measuring the benefits of an investment project. But as Donahue points out in his discussion of the Mercedes investment in Alabama, reasonable estimates of those benefits fail to produce much support for the hypothesis that the cost to Alabama of the incentives given to Mercedes exceeds the benefit to Alabama of Mercedes' investment. One cannot say Alabama would have been economically better off if it had allowed Mercedes to invest elsewhere. All one can say is that Alabama would have been better off if it had attracted the same investment with a less costly package of incentives.

This is certainly not to say that there are no incentives packages whose costs do not exceed, even grossly exceed, the economic benefits to the host economy from the investment project attracted. There must be many. The Mahindra-Ford investment in India is one, at least according to the authors of the report prepared on India for this study; others might include the 1996 Mercedes and Renault investments in Brazil, or the Hyundai semi-conductor investment in Scotland, for example. The point is simply that the evidence does not allow us to conclude that policy competition to attract corporate investment seems, on the whole today, to have pushed the direct costs of policies to attract FDI, and real investment as a whole, beyond the benefits to be derived by host economies from attracting it — either in developing and emerging economies, or in OECD countries.

What the evidence clearly does suggest, on the other hand, is that policy competition is allowing investors to increase their share of the benefits to be derived from their investments, including the spillover benefits, to the host economy. In some cases, undoubtedly, that share approaches, and may exceed, the actual spillover benefits that would have gone to the host economy (i.e. the incentives package has a negative return for the host economy). What the evidence also suggests is that the uncertainty surrounding the economic effects of policy competition has allowed policy makers considerable scope for pursuing that competition. It raises serious questions about the rationale for pursuing policies that cannot be subject to serious evaluation.

Positive-sum Game or Negative-sum Game?

What light does the evidence shed, then, on the effects of policy competition according to the positive-sum-game and negative-sum-game hypotheses presented in Chapter 1? The evidence seems, above all, inconsistent with the stronger (or more extreme) versions of *both* hypotheses. It does not lend much support to the view of the positive-sum-game hypothesis that policy competition for FDI is providing a major effective inducement for governments to pursue actions that significantly enhance local productivity growth, such as investing in education and modern infrastructure — actions which governments would not have pursued in the absence of competition for FDI. Nor does the evidence suggest that policy competition is a major contributor to increasing the global supply of corporate investment and FDI. It is equally true, however, that the evidence does not lend much support to the view of the negative-sum-game hypothesis that competition among governments for FDI is provoking widespread or uncontrolled bidding wars that are pushing investment incentives far above any level that could be socially justifiable. Nor does it support the view that such competition is driving a "race to the bottom" in governments' willingness or ability to regulate markets, including the protection of workers' rights and the defence of labour and environmental standards.

At the same time, however, the evidence provides some support for *milder* versions of *both* hypotheses. It suggests that the competition for FDI in which many sub-national governments are engaging is helping to stimulate the modernisation of, and "better government" by, many of those governments. Policy competition is also part of a broad process of political democratisation of vital importance in some countries, and is helping to stimulate *open* regionalisation in many parts of the world. Nor should its contribution to stimulating governments to enhance local supplies of infrastructure and education be belittled, even if that contribution must be kept in proper perspective.

On the negative side, policy competition has produced bidding wars for some large projects, and can be expected to continue to do so, with the result that a socially sub-optimal share of the spillover benefits from FDI may go to the host economy. Closely related to this distributional effect is the tendency for policy competition to "co-opt" regional development policies, to varying degrees, and to exacerbate rather than ameliorate income inequalities. Also related is the tendency for policy competition to favour large firms at the expense of smaller firms.

The overriding problem with policy competition, however, is its lack of transparency. While some of the reasons governments and investors cite for keeping their deals secret may be accepted as legitimate, that secrecy still creates significant possibilities for graft, corruption and many other types of rent-seeking behaviour. In doing so, it works against the development of competitive markets — whose price signals, based on healthy price competition, are an important part of the very *foundation* for economic and social development that remains fragile or underdeveloped in many developing and emerging economies. It also tends to work against the development of a modern state, sound policy-making and accountable government. It can be seen as the ultimate "distortion", one which ultimately penalises competitive firms, both foreign and local. Its cost to developing and emerging economies, though impossible to measure, can thus be very high. It can be seen as working against the very process of development.

Policy Implications

The key *international* policy question this study set out to address is whether the prisoner's-dilemma nature of competition among governments to attract FDI (and to attract real corporate investment as a whole) calls for collective action by governments to limit either the competition or the negative effects of that competition. For governments in developing and emerging economies, especially those with a federal structure, as for those in OECD countries, a related question is whether action is required to limit policy competition, or its negative effects, among sub-national governments.

The findings of this study point above all to the issue of transparency, on the one hand, and to the relevance for policy makers of the concept of bounded competition, on the other. On both accounts the issue is as much, or more, a matter for national governments to address, as it is a matter for international action. It concerns developing and emerging countries, but also OECD countries.

The transparency issue stems from the significant danger policy competition creates of graft, corruption and rent-seeking behaviour. It raises the delicate question of how to ensure the *accountability* of government officials, particularly those involved in the negotiation of incentives, and points up the need for governments to be able to monitor their own use of incentives. That monitoring could in turn constitute the needed basis for co-operation among governments to ensure that competition for FDI does not lead to costly beggar-thy-neighbour policy wars or incentives wars.

The concept of bounded competition is useful because it constitutes the right objective for governments to pursue in their management of policy competition. An outright suppression of such competition internationally, as a whole, is neither feasible nor necessarily desirable. Allowing it to degenerate into what can easily become predatory competition must also be excluded.

The European experience is rich in potential policy lessons on both accounts. It illustrates the transparency value of financial as opposed to fiscal incentives: financial incentives, especially capital grants, are visible and easy to understand for potential investors; they are flexible and relatively easy to administer for governments; and they are relatively easy to monitor for the supervisory body (in this case the Commission). The EU approach to disciplining incentives, and to addressing the prisoner's-dilemma nature of policy competition, appears to have worked reasonably well because it provides a regulatory framework; within that framework it provides some measure of autonomy for governments that wish to offer incentives (at the national and sub-national level) but it also provides some autonomy for the supervisory body; and it establishes procedures for enforcement and sanctions, which are backed by provisions for judicial review. As the authors of the report on policy competition in Europe prepared for this study note, all in all over the last 40 years, the EU approach has had considerable success in international policy co-ordination and co-operation. It adds up to a system that is unique in international law, one that has no parallel even in countries with federal structures.

The European experience highlights another finding of this study with important policy implications as well. Most competition for FDI among governments, both national and sub-national, internally and internationally, involves competition among investment sites *within* regions. While Singapore may increasingly find itself competing with OECD countries, and one finds a few other examples of inter-regional competition, they constitute exceptions to the overwhelming tendency for competition to occur within rather than between regions — mainly among neighbours. This pattern clearly points to the potential value of regional integration agreements, not only as a policy instrument for attracting FDI, but as an appropriate venue for enhancing international co-operation to limit the potential negative effects of policy competition.

This potential value of regional integration agreements in the realm of FDI policy (visible in Mercosur, NAFTA and elsewhere, as well as in Europe) also brings up the broader issue of incentives-based versus rules-based means of attracting FDI. While much of the debate focuses on the dangers of incentives bidding-wars and downward pressures on labour and environmental standards, it is important to highlight the advantages of rules-based approaches to attracting FDI that do not weaken environmental and labour standards — rules-based approaches that involve creating more stable, predictable and transparent rules for investors and governments alike.

Indeed, as one might infer from Argentina's experience since 1991, for example, or from the U.S. federal government's experience over many years (and from such counter examples as China or India, not to mention Russia), the most effective "policy" to attract FDI is undoubtedly a rules-based one that establishes a high degree of stability, predictability and transparency in the rules governing corporate investment (foreign and domestic) backed by a high degree of credibility gained through an established "track record". Nothing, of course, can substitute for having a large market with promising growth potential — which again points up the potential value of regional integration — along with political and macroeconomic stability (the fundamentals). However, beyond the fundamentals, rules-based approaches to attracting FDI that emphasise stability, predictability, and build on (and add to) a government's credibility can be the most effective long-term basis for attracting the kinds of investment governments most want to attract.

Such rules-based approaches to attracting FDI are also, it must be emphasised, the best way to address the key issue of transparency. A strong rules-based approach can provide the transparency necessary to limit rent-seeking behaviour that can otherwise be so damaging to the very process of development.

Rules-based approaches can also, of course, be combined with the use of incentives, as in Singapore for example. But for many countries, especially those with federal systems, and those that have recently moved, or begun to move, from relatively *dirigiste* systems, the national (i.e. central or federal) government, at least, would be well advised to avoid the use of incentives as a whole.

Equally important, and less obvious perhaps, is the need for a strong judicial system to work in tandem with a strong rules-based approach to attracting real investment. A strong and independent (hence credible) judicial system is what many corporate investors still find lacking in many developing and emerging economies. While it is important for all investors, it can be particularly important for investors that wish to transfer more advanced technologies or knowledge-based assets — precisely the kind of investors and assets many of those countries are most eager to attract.

Two final observations concern the importance of government actions to enhance domestic productivity growth, in the short and long term, as a means to attract FDI. The first refers again to the issue of government actions to enhance local supplies of human resources and modern, well-functioning infrastructure. While the empirical findings of this study do not provide strong support for the hypothesis that intensifying competition for FDI *per se* is leading governments to increase the flow of public and private resources needed to significantly enhance the quantity and quality of these public goods, our findings do largely support the hypothesis that significantly enhancing the availability of human resources and modern infrastructure can, indeed, act as a powerful attraction to corporate investors if (but only if) the "fundamentals" are sound. Policy makers should never lose sight of this fact — even if the visible payoff (including, therefore, the political payoff) often tends, unfortunately, to be longer than the election cycle.

The other observation concerns the importance of *competition policy* (not the same thing, it should be noted, as policy competition) for developing and emerging economies today. In several of those countries, the privatisation of previously state-owned enterprises has accounted for significant FDI inflows in recent years, and in some cases the transaction has involved converting what was a public monopoly into a private one. In some cases the sale price (and value of the FDI inflow) even reflected an engagement by the seller to preserve or protect the monopoly situation of the enterprise through regulatory or other means. The issue, however, is much broader than the matter of privatisation or the transformation of public monopolies into private ones. It reflects the fact that monopolistic or oligopolistic power structures prevail in many developing and emerging economies — as reflected in their economic, political and social structures and institutions — and that those power structures can greatly hinder long-term development. It is in this context that the need for major market-friendly economic reforms which greatly enhance the price competition faced by large firms (be they local or foreign-owned firms) in the local market, and the need as well for major political reforms to enhance and consolidate the institutions of democracy and good government, take on great importance.

It is also in this context that a country's opening up to FDI can be seen as a means for the country to enhance local competition, as well as to gain access to foreign technology, management know-how, finance, etc. FDI can indeed contribute to strengthening such competition, but it can also have the opposite effect. There is nothing automatic or inherent in FDI to ensure that it will enhance local competition. As large numbers of governments in developing and emerging economies move to attract FDI with a vigour virtually unheard of only a few years ago (outside, perhaps, Singapore) — and do so in a context of vigorous globalisation, with many also pursuing far-reaching domestic economic and political reforms to modernise their societies — the development of vigorous competition policy has thus become indispensable to policy reform in developing and emerging economies.

Summing Up

For developing and emerging economies, whose scarce financial resources often push them into a heavy use of fiscal incentives to attract FDI, it is important to stress the value of moving away from incentives-based means towards greater use of domestic and international *rules-based* means of attracting FDI, while maintaining or strengthening their defence of workers' rights and the environment. Strengthening the domestic judiciary system, and domestic competition policy, should be a central part of such a move. Transparency should be one of its objectives.

The prisoner's-dilemma nature of competition for FDI creates a permanent risk of costly beggar-thy-neighbour bidding wars and downward pressures on environmental and labour standards that cannot fully be addressed by national governments in the absence of international policy co-ordination. The secrecy that tends to surround policy competition, especially incentives-based competition, carries major risks for developing and emerging economies as well.

Most competition for *real* corporate investment — as distinct from competition for portfolio or other essentially *financial* investment flows, which is the subject of the OECD report on *Harmful Tax Competition*[3] — occurs within the world's major regions rather than between them. International policy co-ordination to limit the potential damage of competition for FDI is thus most desirable at the regional level, whether that co-ordination is undertaken in conjunction with broader regional-integration agreements or independently. Such regional co-operation could be reinforced by, and/or feed into a process of negotiation of, a broader multilateral agreement on investment.

Notes

1. See note 43 of Chapter 3 for clarification of the difference between the concept of "static" trade diversion (which assumes that countries' production capacities remain constant) and that of "dynamic" trade diversion (which relaxes that assumption).

2. The Clinton administration's legislative proposal of March 1999 to give "NAFTA parity" to the 24 Caribbean and Central American countries that participate in the US Caribbean Basin Initiative, notably as regards parity on trade in textile and apparel products, is an attempt to help redress this problem as part of the process leading to negotiation of the Free Trade Agreement of the Americas (FTAA), to be created by 2005. (See also note 46 of Chapter 3.)

3. OECD (1998).

Bibliography

AHARONI, Y. (1966), *The Foreign Investment Decision Process*, Harvard Business School, Boston.

AHMED, A. and F. ROOT (1978), "The Influence of Policy Instruments on Manufacturing Direct Foreign Investment in Developing Countries" *in Journal of International Business Studies*.

BACHTLER, J. *et al.* (1998), "Policy Competition and Foreign Direct Investment in Europe", mimeo.

BARTIK, T.J. (1994), "Jobs, Productivity and Local Economic Development" *in National Tax Journal*, December.

BIRDSALL, N. and D. WHEELER (1992), "Trade Policy and Industrial Pollution in Latin America: Where are the Pollution Havens" *in* P. LOW (ed.).

BLÖMSTROM, M. and A. KOKKO (1996), "Multinational Corporations and Spillovers", CEPR Discussion Paper No. 1365.

CAMPOS, J. (1998), "Argentina: Government Policies to Attract FDI", mimeo.

CASTLEMAN, B. (1979), "The Export of Hazardous Industries to Developing Countries" *in International Journal of Health Services*, No. 9.

CHEN, E. (1998), "Policy Competition and Foreign Direct Investment in China: The Cases of Three Provinces", mimeo.

CHIA, S.Y. (1998), "Foreign Investment Policy Competition — Singapore", mimeo.

CHRISTIE, I. and H. ROLFE with R. LEGARD (1995), *Cleaner Production in Industry*, Policy Studies Institute, London.

CHUDNOVSKY, D., A. LÓPEZ and F. PORTA (1997), "Market or Policy Driven? The Foreign Direct Investment Boom in Argentina", Oxford Development Studies, Vol. 25, No. 2.

COMMISSION OF THE EUROPEAN COMMUNITIES (1998), "Guidelines on National Regional Aid", CEC, Brussels.

COMMISSION OF THE EUROPEAN COMMUNITIES (1996), *Taxation in the European Union: Report on the Development of Tax Systems*, Brussels, 22 October.

DA MOTTA VEIGA, P. and R. IGLESIAS (1998), "Policy Competition and Foreign Direct Investment in Brazil", mimeo.

DONAHUE, J. (1998), "Subnational Business-Attraction Policies in the United States", mimeo.

DROUIN, M.J. and B. BRUCE-BRIGGS (1978), *Le Canada a-t'il un avenir? : regard sur l'avenir économque politique et social,* Institut Hudson du Canada, Stanke, Montreal.

DUCHIN, F. *et al.* (1995), "Technological Change, Trade and the Environment" *in Ecological Economics*, Vol. 14.

ESTY, D. and M. CHESTOW (eds) (1997), *Next Generation Environmental Policy,* Yale University Press, New Haven.

ESTY, D. and R. MENDELSOHN (1995), *Powering China: The Environmental Implications of China's Economic Growth*, Yale Center for Environmental Law and Policy, New Haven.

FISHER, P. and A. PETERS (1998), *Industrial Incentives: Competition Among American States and Cities*, Upjohn Institute, Kalamazoo.

GENTRY, B. and L. FERNANDEZ (1976), *Survey on Corporate Valuation and the Environment,* Office of Development Studies, UNDP, New York.

HU, Angang (1998), "Comments on Foreign Direct Investment in China", mimeo, Beijing.

ILO (1998*a*), *Labour and Social Issues relating to Export Processing Zones*, ILO, Geneva.

ILO (1998*b*), Committee on Freedom of Association, *Report*, ILO, Geneva, November.

JOHNSTON, D.C. (1995), "Boom Seen in State and Local Tax Aid to Business" *in The New York Times*, September 21.

KPMG PEAT MARWICK LLP, BUSINESS INCENTIVES GROUP (1995), "Business Incentives and Tax Credits: A Boon for Business or Corporate Welfare?", KPMG Peat Marwick, New York, September.

KRUGMAN, P. and E. GRAHAM (1989), *Foreign Direct Investment in the United States*, Institute for International Economics, Washington, D.C.

KUO, W.J. and S.H. CHEN (1998), "Policy Competition and Foreign Direct Investment [in Chinese Taipei]", mimeo.

LAWRENCE, R. (1996), *Single World, Divided Nations? International Trade and OECD Labor Markets*, OECD Development Centre and Brookings Institution Press, Paris and Washington, D.C.

LOW, P. (ed.) (1992), *International Trade and the Environment*, World Bank, Washington, D.C.

LUCAS, R., D. WHEELER and H. HETTIGE (1992), "Economic Development, Environmental Regulation and International Migration of Toxic Pollution, 1960-1988" *in* P. LOW (ed.) (1992).

MANDEL-CAMPBELL, A. (1998), "Contract? What Contract" *in Business Week*, July 27, p. 34.

MORTIMORE, M. and W. PERES (1998), *Policy Competition for Foreign Direct Investment in the Caribbean Basin: Costa Rica, The Dominican Republic and Jamaica*, U.N. Economic Commission for Latin America and the Caribbean (Production, Productivity and Management Division), Santiago.

Mowry, D. (1990), "The National Level Roots of the Failure of State Industrial Policy" *in* E. Yanarella and W. Green.

Nowicki, L. (1998), "Second Generation EPZs and the East Asian Firm" *in* D. Chang and S.M. Lee (eds), Restructuring the Asian-Pacific Economic Systems Towards the 21st Century, Pan-Pacific Business Association, Seoul, Korea.

Noyola, P. and J.E. Espinosa (1998), "Policy Competition and Foreign Direct Investment: The Case of Mexico", mimeo.

OECD (1998), *Harmful Tax Competition: An Emerging Global Issue*, Paris.

OECD (1997a), *Globalisation and Environment: Preliminary Perspectives*, Paris.

OECD (1997b), *The OECD Environment Industry: Situation, Prospects and Government Policies*, Paris.

OECD (1996), *Trade, Employment and Labour Standards*, Paris.

OECD (1994), *The OECD Jobs Study*, Paris.

Oman, C. (1996a), *The Policy Challenges of Globalisation and Regionalisation,* Policy Brief No. 11, OECD Development Centre, Paris.

Oman, C. (1996b), "The Contribution of Competition Policy to Economic Development" *in Competition Policy: 1994 Workshop with the Dynamic Non-Member Economies*, OECD, Paris.

Oman, C. (1994), *Globalisation and Regionalisation: the Challenge for Developing Countries*, OECD Development Centre, Paris, 1994.

Oman, C. (ed.) (1984a), *New Forms of International Investment in Developing Countries: The National Experience*, OECD Development Centre, Paris.

Oman, C. (1984b), *New Forms of Investment in Developing Countries*, OECD Development Centre, Paris.

Pang, Eng Fong (1984), "Foreign Indirect Investment in Singapore" *in* C. Oman (ed.) (1984).

Peres, W. (1990), *From Globalisation to Regionalisation: The Mexican Case*, Technical Paper No. 24, OECD Development Centre, Paris, August.

Peters, A. and P. Fisher (1997), "Do High Unemployment States Offer the Biggest Business Incentives?" *in Economic Development Quarterly*.

Raynauld, A. and F. Raynauld (1998), "L'État-providence des entreprises : les politiques canadiennes de promotion de l'investissement direct étranger", mimeo.

Raynauld, A. and J.P. Vidal (1998), *Labour Standards and International Competitiveness: A Comparative Analysis of Developing and Industrialised Countries,* Edward Elgar, Cheltenham (UK) and Northampton, MA (USA).

Repetto, R. (1995), *Jobs, Competitiveness and Environmental Regulations: What are the Real Issues?,* World Resources Institute, Washington, D.C.

Reuber, G. *et al.* (1973), *Private Foreign Investment in Development,* Clarendon Press for the OECD Development Centre, Oxford.

ROBBINS, D. (1996), *Evidence on Trade and Wages in the Developing World*, Technical Paper No. 119, OECD Development Centre, Paris.

RODRIK, D. (1997), *Has Globalisation Gone Too Far?*, Institute for International Economics, Washington, D.C.

RODRIK, D. (1996), "Labor Standards in International Trade: Do They Matter and What do We Do About Them?", paper prepared for the Overseas Development Council, mimeo, February.

SCHMIDHEINEY, S. and B. GENTRY (1997), "Privately Financed Sustainable Development" *in* D. ESTY and M. CHESTOW (eds).

SIEH LEE, M.L. (1998), "Competing for Foreign Direct Investment: The Case of Malaysia", mimeo.

TAN, S.E. and M. KULASINGHAM (1984), "The Malaysian Experience with New Forms of Investment" *in* C. OMAN (ed.).

TOBEY, J. (1990), "The Effects of Domestic Environmental Policies on Patterns of World Trade" *in Kyklos*, Vol. 43, Autumn.

UNCTAD, *World Investment Report 1998*, Geneva, 1998.

UNCTAD, *World Investment Report 1997*, Geneva, 1997.

UNCTAD, Division on Transnational Corporations and Investment (1996), *Incentives and Foreign Direct Investment*, Current Studies, Series A, No. 30, New York and Geneva.

UNCTAD (1993), *Environmental Management in Transnational Corporations*, Unctad, New York.

VENKATESAN, R. *et. al.* (1998), "Policy Competition Among States in India for Attracting Direct Investment", mimeo.

WEIGEL, D., N. GREGORY and D. WAGLE (1997), *Foreign Direct Investment: The Lessons of History*, Foreign Investment Advisory Service (FIAS) and the International Finance Corporation (IFC) of the World Bank Group, Washington, D.C.

WOOD, A. (1994), *North-South Trade, Employment and Inequality*, Clarendon Press, Oxford.

WORLD BANK (1997), *India 1997 Economic Update: Sustaining Rapid Growth*, Washington, D.C.

WORLD WIDE FUND FOR NATURE (1998), "Pollution Havens: Examining the Evidence and Redefining the Problem", WWF-UK Discussion Paper (mimeo).

YANARELLA, E. and W. GREEN (1990), *The Politics of Industrial Recruitment: Japanese Automobile Investment and Economic Development in the American States*, Greenwood Press, Westport, CT.

OECD PUBLICATIONS, 2, rue André-Pascal, 75775 PARIS CEDEX 16
PRINTED IN FRANCE
(41 2000 03 1 P) ISBN 92-64-17197-5 – No. 50157 2000